An Aspect of Fear

GRACE SHEPPARD

Foreword by the Archbishop of Canterbury

Darton, Longman and Todd
London

First published in 1989 by
Darton, Longman and Todd Ltd
89 Lillie Road, London SW6 1UD

Reprinted 1989

British Library Cataloguing in Publication Data

Sheppard, Grace
  An aspect of fear.
  1. Christian life. Fear
  I. Title
  248'.4

ISBN 0-232-51828-9

Phototypeset by Input Typesetting Ltd, London SW19 8DR
Printed and bound in Great Britain by
Courier International Ltd, Tiptree, Essex

To David, my husband,
for being there,
and for sharing the risks

Contents

Foreword

Many of us know Grace Sheppard as 'good company'. This book introduces us to something of the cost behind it. It should enlarge our understanding of ourselves and our appreciation of her.

It is commonly believed that to show vulnerability causes loss of respect and love amongst those around us. The prospects of such a loss can make us determined to go to almost any lengths to hide our fearful other selves, even from those closest to us. It is for this reason that I believe that this remarkable book is a record of astonishing courage and confidence. Grace has chosen to meet her own fears by placing them at our service. This is a most generous act of trust.

Here we read of her own battle with fear. She tells her story with arresting fluency. The detail is literally painstaking; the analysis direct. Although the problem she addresses is one which may reach its most acute form in what are known as public figures, it is also true that each one of us has a protective public face upon which we may rely too much. This book confirms the lighthearted wisdom expressed by W. H. Auden earlier this century when he said that

> Private faces in public places
> Are wiser and nicer
> Than public faces in private places.

I am sure that many will be grateful to Grace for writing this book and will come to share my appreciation of her, an appreciation that has grown by learning something of her experience and a little more about myself.

Robert Contrans

Preface

'Somehow, we have not been encouraged to talk about it before.' This remark, by a shopkeeper in Dunoon, sums up what I believed before setting out to write about the subject of fear. I chose this subject because it is one I am familiar with and, by facing it over the years, I have come to realise that it is not only a human response that we all share as human beings, but an essential one which needs recognising, accepting and managing. Effectively managed, fear ceases to control our actions, and exists to warn us against anything that will destroy our lives. Ignored or unacknowledged, fear takes control and we find ourselves caught up in varying degrees of destructive behaviour, which can lead to emotional or physical violence.

My fear was largely unacknowledged until I developed agoraphobia, which made me feel like a prisoner in my own body, unable to leave the comfort of my own home or trust other people for long. This happened a long time ago, and was triggered by a severe attack of chicken pox as a newly married young woman. Facing fear squarely, and with professional help, I discovered how to manage it. Now, nearly thirty years later, I have, through a combination of factors, found a wholeness that is distinct from the independent perfection I had been seeking before. These factors included patient love and acceptance from my family and friends, a willingness to be helped by professionals, a belief that God was in it all somewhere, and sheer determination to find a way through. It is a wholeness that I have to go on seeking.

This discovery has made me so grateful for the invitation to write a book, as I have something important to share which I am confident will touch people where they are, especially if they are living with private and uncontrolled fear. 'Wholeness' is another word for 'salvation', and for me everything began to fall into place when I discovered that being saved did not mean being perfect, but rather was a process that we can share in now with our Creator God who knows how we are made, and does not blame us for not getting it right first time. Feeling guilty for being afraid means that a profound theological misunderstanding has grown up which needs to be corrected. God loves us just as we are, fears and all, which does not mean that we have no need to change. Instead, when the knowledge that we are loved so much sinks in, this motivates us to want to change, especially when we find we are hurting ourselves or other people, or spoiling our created world of nature. Knowledge of this love helps us to feel less alone, and more confident in sharing our humanity with others. We become less withdrawn and defensive, and instead more open and alive to one another.

It is all right to be afraid, but not all right to let it do the driving.

My hope and prayer for this book is that it will bring the comfort that I have experienced to all those who feel so uncomfortable with themselves that they are afraid of the fear inside them and pretend it isn't there. I hope that they will find the courage to take a good look at it, be thankful for it, and then learn to drive it. Of course it is a risky way to live, but far more exciting and far more creative than wasting away in private and increasing terror, or frightening each other with warnings of constant danger. But it takes time and patience, and we cannot do it alone. We need each other's love and acceptance; so, while working at our own salvation, we can offer this acceptance to another, just as Christ loved us, while knowing the love of his Father, and ours.

While creating this book, I have shared the experience with a number of people. They have not only demonstrated their support of me as a person by being there, but also by offering their skills. I am deeply grateful to them for enabling me to bring this to birth with so much conviction and enjoyment, alongside the labour and the pain. From each of them I have received constant encouragement, absolute trust and truthfulness.

They include my husband, David Sheppard, my daughter,

PREFACE

Jenny Sinclair, and my parents, Bryan and Eleanor Isaac; my readers, Pat Starkey, Richard Buck, Hanna McCluskey and Mark Boyling; my editors from Darton, Longman and Todd, Teresa de Bertodano and Sarah Baird-Smith; Margaret Funnell, who typed and copied the heaps of paper, and Cynthia Miller and George Walker who sustained the home-base during my absence; Godfrey and Lesley Butland for being the first to encourage me after reading the original synopsis, and Derek Worlock and all at Archbishop's House for providing me with an uninterrupted place and gracious hospitality, where I revised the final draft; the people of the village of Cairndow whose lives provided constant friendship and encouragement when I first settled down to write, and the people from the Liverpool Diocese for their acceptance and support through their prayers and interest; all those whose stories appear in this book, and for their willingness for them to be included. Last but not least, I am grateful to two authors: Gerard Hughes, whose book, *God of Surprises* (DLT) introduced a note of tenderness into my understanding of God at the right time, and Bishop John V. Taylor, whose *A Matter of Life and Death* (SCM Press) continually inspires me to choose life with all its natural responses.

February 1989   *Grace Sheppard*

1

To be Afraid is Human

I stopped by the fire extinguisher, looking desperately for
somewhere to sit down. My legs had turned to jelly and my
heart was beating fit to burst. The underground station at
Holborn seemed a lonely place though it was teeming with
people. I thought I was dying. In a last-ditch throw for
survival, I turned to the next person hurrying to catch a train.
'Excuse me, could you help? I feel awful; I don't know what's
happening.' My breath was coming in short gasps and my
chest felt bound with chains. My helper offered his arm and
suggested we went up for some fresh air. With difficulty we
reached the top of the escalator and looked for a taxi. Frightened to be left on my own, I clung on to my sanity; I felt I
was hovering between two worlds. On the one hand was the
world of the city pavements of London, and on the other, my
private internal world, which was in turmoil. My brain was
full of fluttering butterflies and my heart was racing at an
alarming rate. If I let go now, I thought, I'm finished; I'm
as good as dead. Alone and helpless, I prayed the 'Lord help
me' kind of prayer. I was terrified. I had come to the end of
my own resources.

Then miraculously, a taxi drew up and two people inside
it called my name. Blinded with panic, I could not see who
they were. But they persevered, and kept on calling. They
were from my newly adopted church, St Mary's in Islington,
where my husband was a curate. Gratefully I climbed aboard,
and tried to explain. We decided to go to the Medical Centre,
where I hoped I would find our doctor.

Eventually a doctor arrived. Lying flat, shaking violently
from head to toe, I repeated the name of Jesus; I hoped that

this would somehow fend off my terror that I was taking leave of my senses. I felt in danger. I thought of my husband, preaching that evening in St Paul's Cathedral, miles out of reach. The doctor was perplexed; I was encouraged to go home to bed, rest, and wait for his visit in the morning.

I cannot remember how I reached home. Although it was a relief to be among familiar objects, even the pillows did not feel really comfortable. Still shaking violently, and sweating profusely, I longed for David's return. I was overcome with the pervading guilt that I had done wrong by losing control like this. Surely I should be able to pull myself together. But I could not. Together with the shaking, the uncertainty and the guilt, there was an underlying, multi-faceted dread. First I dreaded losing my mind. Then I fancied that my new husband would tire of me. We had been married for three months, and already I felt apologetic; I was a nuisance, a hindrance. I feared my faith was slipping; even God did not seem to be there. As I frightened myself further with fantasies, I felt sorry to be human.

Leaning back on my pillow, feeling adrift and alone, I searched the last few months for clues to the cause of my condition. It was a time of great confusion. With hindsight I would not have had far to look for the trigger. Only three months earlier we had flown off to Italy on honeymoon after our wedding, carefree and contented. Sun, sand and good beaches were in abundance and, deeply happy, we began to relax. We were full of plans for the future, and quite unaware of the traumas in store.

It was hectic before the wedding. As well as the preparations for the important day, and visits to each other's relations, we were to move. Some time earlier, David had been approached by the Bishop of Barking, Hugh Gough, to be the Warden of the Dockland Settlement in Canning Town, which later came to be known as the Mayflower Family Centre. We made the decision to go there in June. That month, on the nineteenth, we were married.

The country was in the middle of a heatwave. It was the

height of the cricket season. But over the small picturesque village of Lindfield in Sussex, the heavens opened, and there was a freak rain storm. The cartwheel hats and flimsy dresses of some of our guests went limp, and we appeared from the church under two huge umbrellas. But nothing could quench our enthusiasm and joy; we had waited fifteen months for this day, and were longing to go into partnership together. I felt ready for anything.

The job that David had been invited to do was a sizeable one and involved a variety of gifts, not least resilience and a pioneering spirit. We both had youth on our side, and between us a variety of experience. I was a clergyman's daughter, and a trained primary school teacher. My home had been a place where I learned that Christian service did not begin and end in the local situation, and I had relations in the overseas mission field. I could play the piano and sing; I was fit and athletic. I was looking forward to bringing what I could to the job in hand. But before we could begin our work, we needed a good break and the chance to be private people.

Once in Italy, we began to explore. Quite soon, while driving to Florence, I had begun to feel uncomfortable, and knew that all was not well. Putting it down to post-wedding-itis, and unaccustomed heat, I did not fret unduly. And then I came out in spots. We called the doctor, who diagnosed chicken-pox. At first it was funny. And then reality began to dawn; the spots were an interruption to our romantic interlude. I began to feel anxious, and then anxiety gave way to deeper fears.

It had been hard enough to find a date for the wedding, as David's schedule was tight, and he would have to get back. Separation threatened and, on doctor's instructions, I packed my things, and moved into a hospital in Rapallo. David stayed on at the hotel for a day or two; after such a short time together, we were apart.

I felt ugly with these spots, and afraid that David would grow tired of me. Neither he nor I had bargained for this crude interruption. So, afraid that he might not love me with spots like this, I set out to forestall this nightmare by protect-

3

ing him, suggesting that he leave me to recover on my own, and return to work. In stoic fashion, I persuaded him that I could manage alone, and that he was not to worry. His first engagement was an important cricket match, and my pride would not allow anyone to think I had prevented him from playing. I had experience as a bossy elder sister; I insisted, and finally he agreed he wanted to get back, and that there was little he could usefully do by just being there. Leaving me in the hands of the nuns, who had showed great kindness, he set off for home, alone.

So I began my traumatic sojourn in the Italian hospital. The chicken pox was severe, and there was talk of smallpox. I was moved into isolation in the bowels of the hospital. I felt cut off. I didn't speak Italian, and I was a long way from the telephone. Bars at my windows emphasised my isolation. After David had left, the nuns visited me less frequently. This time I would have to cope alone.

I wrote letters home. Anxious not to worry my new husband any more, I did not mention feeling lonely, miserable or ill. Making the best of my circumstances meant covering up the truth, joking about the huge red, yellow and green pills, referring to them as traffic lights. I drew a picture of the view outside my window which was of a tree in a courtyard bathed in Italian sunshine. But I left out the bars. I tried to thank God that things were not worse, and dreamed of returning home. I was afraid to admit to my lonely feelings.

I was not, however, totally alone. Further along the passage was another woman. She called out, day and night, beating on her door and crying, *'Perché?'* ('Why?'). She was locked in and quite demented. Her cries frightened me. Her questioning was too close to mine for comfort, and I tried to shut it out by blocking my ears.

I discovered later that David had tried to telephone me, but his attempts were frustrated. Eventually, his first letter arrived, and I read it over and over.

Then the spots began to subside. I became very impatient, and determined to leave at the earliest possible moment. All my hitherto persuasive powers failed with the doctors, who insisted I stayed until the last spot had disappeared. Despite this, I began to prepare for the journey home.

This time I knew I needed help. During my stay in hospital I received one visitor, an Anglican priest, who was on holiday locally. He was clearly afraid of catching my infection. With one finger on the door handle, he would open the door and hastily sit on a chair in the furthest corner of my room. Sometimes he would climb up on to the wall outside, hanging on to the bars, and hand books through the window for me to read. It was he who made arrangements for me to travel. I was grateful for such practical help.

The time came to leave. Seated alone on the train, I settled down for the long journey home. After a while, my excitement died down, and I began to think about crossing Paris. Excitement gave way to panic; I felt I would be unable to find the right station in Paris. I was confused and began to fidget. It seemed that, if I stopped fidgeting, I might turn to stone. I was petrified. I knew I needed help, but did not know what to do. Just then an English family boarded the train. I wondered if they would help me. But first I had to ask. For over an hour I tried to pluck up courage to walk over to them. But I had my pride; I did not want to tell them that I was frightened about crossing Paris. I did not want to look silly. Finally, I went over and asked them if they could help me.

They accepted me easily and graciously, and said they were also crossing Paris and would be glad of the company. Much relieved, I joined them, and we travelled together until I caught the boat train to Victoria where David would be waiting. I felt I owed them my life. Their acceptance of me, asking no questions, making no conditions, arrested the feeling that my blood was freezing in my veins. It enabled me to take courage for the last lap of my journey. So I thanked them and we parted.

Stepping out of the train in my pink going-away outfit, no one could have guessed the nightmare of those days of honeymoon spent apart. David was there at the station, waiting to meet me and we clung to each other. But this joy was short-lived, as the press were also there, wanting pictures of our reunion. So our private joyful meeting turned into a public display of posed kisses from the train window. It was a small price to pay, but already I felt the tension between public and private that we had to learn to manage. However, any feeling that I was a disappointment to David dissolved in our embrace. He was clearly pleased to see me – and we stepped once more into partnership.

Once home, we lost no time in sharing our adventures, glad to be together, privately, at last. It was the beginning of July, and there was plenty to do before leaving our new home in Islington.

On August 1st, David was officially appointed Warden of the Mayflower Family Centre. It had been agreed that he would attend the Centre two days a week, while sustaining his work as curate of St Mary's for the remaining five days. I had given up my teaching some months before, and felt between two worlds, unsure of my role in either.

After Italy, I became easily tired, and the thought of moving again so soon became alarming. David was very busy, and much in demand as a speaker and cricketer. I accompanied him whenever I could. We shared our home – a few rooms – with friends from the parish, and it was also used for meetings. I would wait for his key in the lock around ten o'clock most evenings. Much energy was needed for this new life; but I felt strained and under pressure. I kept up appearances in the parish and further afield; I was afraid to admit my feelings of strain to anyone. I was afraid to stop, and reflect. I didn't want to be a drag on my partner. Underneath I was terrified that I would not measure up to my handsome, energetic, busy husband; I resolved that I would just keep going.

I do not recall why I was in Holborn Underground station. It was there that I collapsed, six weeks after David's appointment to Canning Town, ten weeks after my return from Italy and twelve after our wedding. I was twenty-two years old, and frightened out of my wits. So I waited, trembling, for David to return from St Paul's, feeling ashamed that he should see me like this. This time I had no spots to blame.

6

This time, we would together have to face the fact that I needed help. This time I was incapable of protecting him from my weakness and my humanity. He returned, and we waited for morning, and the doctor's visit.

The doctor came. He referred me to the London Hospital and I was admitted to the heart ward for observation. There was much shaking of heads and puzzlement from the specialists. It was during the 'flu' epidemic of 1957 and wards were bursting with sick people. Opposite me a woman died; the nurses safety-pinned the cubicle curtains as if to shield us from what we already knew. All this time I was short of breath, with a searing pain in my chest, and irregular heartbeats. I was given insulin to get me to eat, as I could not swallow my food. I felt deeply guilty at being ill, holding my new husband back, and frustrated at not knowing what was the matter. 'Nothing organically wrong' was the refrain. I felt dizzy and trapped. I was coming to terms with the fact that I could not cope alone, that I was dependent; but it was proving a hard school. After all, I had managed up until now. So, with mixed feelings, I agreed to see a psychiatrist, for the specialists still could not pin down the cause of my symptoms.

In the past I had had a strong faith which had stood me in good stead. But now somehow I was losing my grip. The awful prospect dawned on me that God might leave me. I dreamed one night that he was holding on to my fingertips; I felt that my hand would slip out of his at any moment. I was very distressed and frightened, and confided this dream to David on one of his frequent visits. He did not appear to be shocked, neither did he offer any magic solutions. Quite calmly he accepted my word and suggested that for the time being I trust in something that I could see and touch. I could trust him. His faith would have to do for both of us. This carried me through that crisis and I did not feel so alone and afraid.

I was referred to a consultant, who made me feel like a rational human being. He suggested that David and I went for a holiday to try to retrieve what we had lost in June. With high hopes we set off for a hotel in the New Forest, but my dizziness, jelly legs and general feeling of fear and foreboding

7

increased. So we returned to the consultant, who until then had suggested that I was making good progress. To our great consternation, he urged a spell as a voluntary patient in the psychiatric unit of Guy's Hospital. I sobbed like a child as I came to accept the reality that I needed more help. It was a letting go, and the beginning of a long climb back towards wholeness. But I did not realise this then; the shame of it took a long time to overcome. I felt an utter failure as a human being and as David's wife. My hard-earned pride had received a body blow and I failed to see how I could maintain any degree of dignity. I had the usual fears: what would everyone think? Would I ever live this down? I felt marked for life. But I knew when I was beaten, and agreed to go.

The idea of entering a psychiatric clinic held untold horrors for me. Certain questions would not leave me. Would I lose my reason, my friends, my husband? Would I be submitted to hypnosis or electrical treatment against my will? Would I really express my anguish in the same noisy way as the woman in the next cubicle to mine had done? So, once more I set about controlling myself as much as I could. I very quickly stated that I did not want hypnosis or electrical treatment. To my amazement and relief my specialist agreed. I gained confidence in him and began to talk freely in psychotherapy sessions; the slow re-building of self-confidence began. I was prescribed quite large amounts of barbiturates. I did not completely cease taking these until twenty years later, even though I had determined to come off them from the moment they were prescribed. From the clinic we were taken on very short walks around Southwark Bridge. I dreaded these and found I had to draw on deep reserves of courage to go; sometimes I needed to cling on to a fence or wall or another person. I was doing so well inside the safety of the clinic that each walk felt like a major set-back.

After seven weeks in the clinic I was discharged and the rest was up to me. It was the winter of 1957. We moved in January 1958 from Islington to the Mayflower. There, we had carved out a flat from the hostel corridor, and put in our own front door. This was the first time a married couple had ever lived there. Soon after the move I remember feeling a tinge of excitement at being a part of this pioneering venture. But when the electrician who came to do some work under the floorboards in our small kitchen asked 'Do you think you're going to like it round here?' I answered 'Yes, the people have been so friendly and helpful, I expect I shall get used to it'. He said, 'You hesitated then.' He had spotted all too quickly my underlying fear that I wasn't going to cope, but he did not know that I could not walk outside my front door unaided. It seemed ludicrous to reflect that here was I, a 22-year-old with limited experience of the world, taking up this new life among people whose ways were so different from all I had ever known.

The Mayflower Family Centre was a mock Tudor complex which included hostel buildings for thirty residents, a church, youth clubs, a nursery school, an open-air playground and an indoor swimming pool. Incongruously, these buildings, set around a courtyard in Cambridge College style, were in the heart of London's dockland. Most of the surrounding houses had been bombed during the last war and cleared, leaving expanses of waste ground where the children played and made bonfires. There were guards on our windows, and we overlooked a scrap-yard and one of the surviving terraced streets.

From the Mayflower buildings we set out to provide a place where local people could come without being patronised, bringing both their talents and their needs. At the same time, we would offer ourselves, by living there, and by bringing our time and varied skills to the provision of a nursery school, youth clubs and legal aid. Having a church also meant that people could come at important moments in their lives to celebrate or to mourn. It was a place for all the family, where we learnt from one another.

David had decided early on that all wives of staff members would be full members of the Staff Team, attend the five-hour staff meeting each week and share in all the responsibilities of our enterprise. Despite my state of health, I was included. It did wonders for my dignity; I felt I had something to offer.

Also, I could provide lunch for the eleven team members – and this held no terrors for me.

But I was too frightened to walk across the courtyard, or into the hostel dining-room or to church without someone else. The usual, uncontrollable, symptoms – wobbly legs, a feeling of unreality, palpitations and acute perspiration – would come over me. The comfort of holding on to someone else's arm, or a piece of furniture, or even a tree, was real – as was the unjudging friendship of a young resident called Peter. When I found enough courage to slip into the club-room converted into a temporary church, he was often on duty; he asked no questions, grinned and let me enter at my own pace. I would sometimes need to stand by the curtain at the back for the whole service. While I was condemning myself as weak and stupid, and a failure, he accepted me without fuss and with good humour. My behaviour didn't appear to worry him, and I liked that. He gave me confidence and the will to fight. There should be Peters in every church.

Travelling in a lift, going in a tunnel or sitting under a hairdrier, I felt suffocated. I could not walk anywhere alone, or go shopping. I could not cross roads or even pass the London Hospital in the car, as the memory of the dying woman was too much and I would feel the suffocation again. It was also very difficult to sit in church without feeling agitated and trapped. I always had a lot of sympathy with the younger members of the congregation who sat at the back whispering and crackling their sweet papers throughout the service. I felt I understood their need to fidget.

In our community we were very exposed to the public. Although many of my fears were private, I felt increasingly able to let some of them be known. Mercifully, not once during those months did anyone tell me to 'snap out of it', or 'pull myself together'.

Many times I puzzled over the meaning of a text I had often quoted, 'I can do all things through Christ who strengthens me.' There is a major problem when you find you can't.

From a very early age, I had come to believe that to be self-sufficient was the height of maturity. Being so young, I wanted to be 'grown up'. However, one of the lessons of those early years in East London was about the need to be interdependent. David and I needed each other, and we also needed the help of others. I had learned a lesson.

The Mayflower was a busy and demanding place. There was a need to break new ground, to go out and meet people in the local community, and also those further afield who would support us with their prayers and with their money. This in turn brought many visitors to the Centre, and gradually the hostel filled with residents coming to live and work in the area for a while, though we always had a rule that local people should come first in our priorities. We were soon a community of thirty people.

As I increased in self-confidence, my visits to the consultant became less frequent. Also, David and I were delighted with the news that I was pregnant. I had a new and welcome feeling of contentment, though underneath I was deeply anxious that I might not be able to love my baby enough. I need not have worried. In the spring of 1962 I gave birth to Jenny. Her arrival brought great rejoicings, and I revelled in being her mother. So we settled down to a new rhythm of life. I had no idea that our horizons would stretch across the world inside the year.

Soon my confidence was to receive another testing. The Mayflower Council had decided that David should take a sabbatical leave; it was seven years since his ordination. He would therefore be available to play for the England Test Team to tour Australia in the autumn. Earlier in the year we had discussed the possibility of going to Australia; inevitably I had a struggle. How could someone who couldn't even cross the road alone contemplate going to Australia? And with a new baby? For ten months? David had declared that he would not go without us. So I discussed my position with a friend, and I made up my mind; the time had come to look forward and face my fears. In July we learned on the radio of David's selection. In October he set off with the team, and Jenny and I followed in November by sea with a friend and colleague from the Mayflower, for I had acknowledged that I would need her help and friendship.

We enjoyed the trip. Jenny was a most contented baby, so

we were able to enjoy her company during the day and to sleep peacefully at night.

Jenny's first birthday was celebrated in the garden of our comfortable rented bungalow on the North Shore in Sydney. We had an excellent base there, though I was daily in dread of sighting the first spider or snake. I became used to lizards on the wall, but that was all. My terror in discovering a tarantula crawling out of my hand while holding a dustpan is vivid to this day. I shook for half an hour. My maternal and protective instincts were at their height, let alone thoughts for my own survival.

Homemaking and mothering were not my only roles. There was a reception at the Archbishop's House for the team and their wives and other distinguished guests. With some excitement and some trepidation I went. To my consternation, our hostess, the Archbishop's wife, announced that no one was to sit next to anyone they knew. Small tables had been laid and we moved obediently to sit with a stranger. But Colin Cowdrey, a real friend, had already taken his place at one of the tables and with a welcoming gesture indicated that I sit at his table, which I did with some relief. I was still on edge; it all seemed so grand compared with life at the Mayflower. Later in the evening my shyness reached its peak when the towering figure of the Prime Minister, Sir Robert Menzies, came towards me. I slunk away behind the piano, unable to speak civilly, totally overwhelmed, and dumb with fear.

There were other occasions when my inexperience and nervousness were confronted. I was afraid of not fitting in, of standing out on public occasions. I like clothes, but I have a dread of not wearing 'the right thing' at public events. One day, arriving in the air-conditioned box in Adelaide to watch a match, I wore a simple summer dress. Jenny was with me in her small pram. To my horror all the other women were wearing not only hats and very smart dresses and jackets, but also little white gloves. Next day, I hastened to the shops to find a couple of suitable hats and some gloves. Later, in Sydney, feeling more confident, and in another dress, I glided in wearing one of my Adelaide purchases, a huge wide-brimmed red straw hat. Unhappily for me, all the other women wore simple summer dresses, and no hats, gloves or even stockings. So my hat went hastily under the chair for the duration of the match. But my face was red.

As the *Canberra* moved out of Sydney Harbour, I was full of relief that I had managed the trip. David had played well, so another anxiety – that I'd be blamed by the press and others for a poor performance – was laid to rest. The great joy was that we were returning home as a family and had four weeks on the boat together. Reflecting during the voyage home, I was glad to have taken the risk of going to Australia, despite the fears. I felt that I had grown.

So we returned to east London and our friends at the Mayflower.

2

Afraid of Dying

With increased confidence I played the piano in chapel, helped prepare candidates for confirmation, and cooked for a cricket tour in Sussex of our local young men from the club. There followed two years of steady development of confidence. Jenny was growing strong and healthy and began at the Mayflower Nursery School when she was three.

Round about this time David and I decided to have a holiday on our own in a cabin cruiser on the Thames. I felt nauseous during that week and had the beginnings of a pain in my right side. When we returned home I went to the doctor, who gave me antibiotics. A fortnight later, the pain had intensified; it was excruciating. I also had to rush embarrassingly to and from the toilet. I feared appendicitis.

The doctor took one look and told me to go to the hospital casualty department. David and Jenny came with me, and we waited for four hours before my name was called. The surgeon on duty at the London Hospital examined me and said I must be admitted immediately. This had become an emergency, so after a family discussion, David left with Jenny and to pack a bag for me. I was being admitted for acute appendicitis.

Hours later I was wheeled into the operating theatre, my fears greatly allayed by discovering that the surgeon was clearly taking my condition seriously. I was in great pain. He operated that night, and while under the anaesthetic, I little knew the problem that he was facing. Here was no burst appendix but a growth which caused the bowel to adhere to the abdominal wall. Another surgeon had to be found to share the decision to remove the growth and proceed with a different operation. David was on the road to Sussex to take Jenny to his mother's, and could not be contacted.

When I woke next morning, I was suspicious. Somehow I did not feel that all was straightforward.

I had to wait seven days for the pathology report, which confirmed the cancer; it had been necessary to remove my ovaries as well. The word 'growth' meant 'cancer', and cancer held only one meaning for me. It spelt death. Strangely I didn't feel afraid at the time; I received the news as a matter of fact. It was only later when a young medical student friend came to visit me and said, 'So you're going down for radiotherapy', that the alarming truth began to dawn. I was afraid of dying. I broke down as I told the ward sister what he had said, and she cried with me. The attention I received from the surgeon and the other staff was total. The surgeon came to my room each evening for half an hour and sat waiting for my questions. He would click his fingers and say, 'Next question'. Gradually my fears began to surface until some time later, with great difficulty, I asked the unaskable: 'Will I ever come out of here alive?' 'Well', he said, 'put it this way, if you were to walk out of your room now and get knocked down by a trolley, break your leg . . . you might not. But if, in a little while, the treatment works, and you're good, then there's a fifty–fifty chance you'll come out alive.'

The next questions were about the treatment.

'Does radiotherapy hurt?' 'No.'

'How long will it take?' 'Not long.'

'Will I be put in a room alone with a machine?' 'Yes.'

'Does everyone wear white gowns like space-people?' 'No.'

'Supposing I panic and want to leave, can I?' 'You won't.' Answers came thick and fast.

The day dawned for my first treatment. I was very anxious. The porter arrived with the wheelchair and blanket and wheeled it to my bed. He'd done this a thousand times. 'Come on, love. Off we go,' he said cheerfully. Gingerly I put my feet on the floor and prepared for a journey into the unknown. 'I mustn't let the side down,' I thought. I sat mutely as we entered the lift. It seemed a long way down. When we arrived at the basement my mouth was dry and my heart was pumping. I didn't like basements; I felt closed in. The huge pipes overhead snaked their way as far as the eye could see, hot and heavy. They reminded me of a recurring nightmare I had as a child when I got caught up in a room of machines before my father stepped in to rescue me in the nick of time. But my father was not with me now. I was an adult and had to rescue myself. And I did not have the strength to jump up and run back through the basement with the everlasting pipes.

At last we arrived in a brightly lit area with two cheerful women in white short-sleeved dresses. They greeted me, and briskly showed me the room with the cobalt machine where I was to be treated. I clambered up and lay down on my back, holding the polyphotos of Jenny, determined to hang on to those.

The machine was lined up and the radiotherapist left the room with a cheerful 'See you in a minute'. And the door closed. There was a whirring sound and the powerful rays were released. I didn't feel a thing. So that was true. I then realised there was nothing I could do but trust the professionals, and lie still. I feared I would fidget or move and be 'done' in the wrong place. Four minutes on each side. Just like a steak. I thought of David and Jenny with gladness, and of the rest of my family. I lifted the polyphotos up and enjoyed the delicious expressions on my daughter's face. The clicking stopped and I was done on one side. The door opened and my reassuring radiotherapist came in to turn me over. It was slightly easier on my front, and the minutes passed more quickly. And then it was over. I'd coped without having hysterics or fainting or going off my head as I'd feared.

Twenty one trips later, I was feeling sick, sore and weak, but there was a sense of achievement which I was glad to experience. And I was not alone. David's daily visits, the friendliness of the porters as they wheeled me down, and the cheerfulness of the hospital staff all helped me to find the courage to face my fears. The prayers, the postcards and the flowers, and the visits from many people filled my room and gave added reason for me to want to live. There were five of us in that ward. I am the only one to have survived.

Through this experience, I continued to learn the lessons of interdependence, and of the need to recognise that we all belong to one another. I became convinced that we're put on this earth not just to battle alone, or even to dole out our favours to others without expecting to receive something in return. Learning to receive became as important as learning to give without counting the cost. I could not have survived if I had refused to receive from countless people in those difficult days. My visitors told me that I sometimes appeared to have more life to give than those outside the hospital who were weary with their independent, lonely lives – I knew this was because I had received so much. Sick people often have that effect. The interaction of giving and receiving is a life-giving activity and one which takes a life-time to practise. It creates new life and fresh energy.

Sitting in bed, surrounded by cards and flowers, and with a stream of visitors I felt I was doing all the receiving. I looked pink and cheerful. But despite appearances, I was struggling with more anxiety. I was afraid that my illness was interfering with David's work. He looked so tired. Nothing, I had thought, should ever interfere with his work, not even my health. His being there most days was a huge commitment, yet he could not know straightaway how important that was to my healing. It is sometimes hard work just being there for someone, especially if our presence does not produce instant and visible results. But who suggested that healing does not involve hard work?

One day I received a special visitor. Jack Wallace, the Chairman of the Mayflower Council, came into my room. He must have noticed that it wasn't one of the good days. Anxious to show that I was not malingering I suppose, I told him how privileged I was to be given all this time to pray for people. He became very indignant. 'Grace,' he said, 'your job is to concentrate on getting well – you leave the rest to us.' I collapsed with tears of relief. Delivered from this battle of prayer, I felt free and almost absolved from guilt; I began to put all my energy into getting well. I was to need plenty when, nearing the end of the course of radiotherapy, I was tempted to quit.

I left the London Hospital for the third and last time, resolved to build on the skill of the staff and the love of my husband, family and friends. I was very weak, and David and I were advised to go away together for my convalescence. His tender loving care, as we inched our way through each day towards my becoming stronger, was infinite. We were very private, and no one knew the extent of his care, except me. By this time Jenny was three and I was missing her. So, after a fortnight in Eastbourne, we returned home and began the long slow climb back to health again. David resumed his work.

Three years later, in 1968, I went on a day's outing to South-end with a coachload of the women from the Mayflower. On the way back, the Mayflower coach, a regular source of amusement, broke down, again, and we had to wait for help. I returned home at 1.30 in the morning to find David still up, and so deathly pale that I thought he was ill. He invited me to sit down and made us a cup of tea, for he had something on his mind he wanted to share.

He had lunched with the Bishop of Southwark, Mervyn Stockwood, whom he had only met once before. We had understood that they were to discuss apartheid and sport. But during the meal the bishop had invited him to consider allowing his name to be put forward as the next Bishop of Woolwich, to follow Dr John Robinson. At the news, my reaction surprised even me. I leapt up and flung my arms round his neck and congratulated him. How marvellous that someone had noticed the quality of his work down here, in the East End of London! I was delighted – it would be a reward for him. But then the reality of the situation began to dawn on me. It would mean moving again, after all this time. We would be much more in the public view and I would be a bishop's wife, whatever that might mean. He would have to wear grand robes, to process in formal church services, and I would have to sit in the front row and be smartly dressed. And what about Jenny, who was six? We would belong to one hundred and fifty parishes instead of one, and

David would be out, travelling a lot. It would mean leaving our East London friends, and that felt like dying a little. There was a lot to think about.

I was sure that David could do the job, but equally sure that I was unsuitable. I felt woefully inadequate. I had come to enjoy the friendliness of the Mayflower and the Canning Town people, and their informality and openness. I felt free and could sit where I liked in church among the people who had so lovingly accepted me through the traumas of recent years. The idea of separating from them permanently became formidable, especially as we had been discussing with the congregation our temporary departure for a year's sabbatical leave in Edinburgh. 'You'll never come back', some folk said.

Then followed four months of discussion, negotiation, and activity as the invitation became firm and the idea of moving jobs became more feasible. Feeling clearly called, and with the congregation's blessing, David accepted the invitation. Plans for Edinburgh were unscrambled, an extended holiday was planned, a house was found and bought in Peckham, and we left Canning Town for the South Bank.

Just before we left, a friend came to visit us. She asked us if we knew anyone, preferably Christian, who could use a Morris 1100, as she was going abroad and wanted to give it to the right person. Astonished, David and I looked at each other, as we had been scanning the papers for a second-hand Morris 1100 for me – it was clear that David's new job would take him away from home much more and I would really need to drive.

I hadn't driven for years and was feeling distinctly nervous at the prospect. London roads were fearsome places, and drivers needed a large supply of self-confidence and assertion to get through. Unsure whether our friend's visit was the answer to this problem, we shared our position with her. 'Marvellous,' she said, 'You're just the kind of person I had in mind!' I decided I would take up driving again. That decision was a major plank in the bridge of confidence that I was building. So the car was handed over and we gave a thank offering to the Mayflower.

I still had agoraphobia. I could not cross the road or walk

far alone without needing to walk by a wall, or hold on to a person or pram. I would feel totally drained after each effort to push the boundaries, and often felt defeated. But the thought of driving made me feel safer.

Being alone in a car became less fearsome than walking round the corner to the shops. I felt protected. It had other, more obvious uses. I am quite a handyman, and the car became very useful when bringing home lengths of hardboard to box in the bath, and carrying rolls of lino to lay in the bathroom. I visited friends and set myself journeys with a 'treat' at the end as a carrot. In this way I became much more aware of progress in mobility, and I was confronting the enforced isolation that most bishops' wives experience when their husbands start work as new bishops after having been in a parish. I began to shop alone, and did not mind driving in the traffic nearly as much as negotiating the terrifying roads on foot. But I was still fearful. If there was a large junction, then I would go a long way round to avoid it. I would often panic at traffic lights, where I was very frightened of losing control of the car and crashing involuntarily.

It was not just my car that helped me feel safer. I began to make new friends. I was able to share my difficulties with a friend who lived in Camberwell. We enjoyed one another's company; we laughed, discussed matters domestic and theological and shared meals together. Not once did I feel patronised by her, or that I was a burden. While sharing at a deep level, we retained a lightness which was life-giving. Learning to make friends became a crucial part of my survival as a private person.

It was important to maintain this ability to laugh as we approached the serious business of deciding whether or not to become a bishop's household. I had a dread of pomposity, and the thought of David in a mitre filled me with mixed feelings.

Just before David agreed to accept the invitation for his name to go forward as bishop, we went to see the play *Hadrian VII*, about the rapid rise of a young priest to bishop, then cardinal, then Pope. Although I was aware that the play depicted a bygone Roman Catholic Church, I became more

20

and more disturbed as the evening progressed. Coming from an evangelical background where church worship was simple and ordinary, I found it hard to imagine being married to someone who would be dressed in scarlet and purple in the name of the Christian Church. As cardinals and bishops came strutting down the aisles capped and mitred and literally brushing our seats with their robes, furious questions arose in me. Was this what I was being asked to subscribe to? Did becoming a bishop mean such a switch from our simple ways of Anglican worship in Canning Town? How would David avoid becoming removed from 'ordinary' people? And what would it all do to me? I have always hated pomposity, although I'm aware it is often a self-defence mechanism.

The play provided a focus for my struggle in leaving the people of Canning Town. Just like Liverpool people, they were quick to spot pretence; they emphasised the importance of being yourself. This play highlighted some of the pressures upon public people in Church and State, and the need for personal integrity and honesty. The jokes from Mayflower people were thinly veiling their anxiety that we might get above ourselves and lose touch with the likes of them. Even close friends became uncertain whether to continue to call us by our Christian names, afraid of showing disrespect.

3

Afraid of Judgement

David was consecrated Bishop of Woolwich on October 18th in Southwark Cathedral. Armed with a packet of chewing gum and dressed in our best, Jenny and I walked down the aisle in the crowded cathedral to take our seats beside the Archbishop's wife, Mrs Ramsey, an easy gentle neighbour. I had thought carefully about whether or not to wear a hat. Finally, I could not bring myself to go out and buy a hat for this occasion when for twelve years I had not worn one in church in Canning Town. The people there had strong views about putting on airs, which I had grown to understand and share. I wanted to keep faith with them, to be myself, and somehow to show them that we would not desert them in this wider responsibility. Church is not a fashion show and so, even though I love hats, I made the small personal statement that day in Southwark Cathedral which was necessary for me in those early days of being more public.

I was miserable during the service. My heart was beating wildly, my hands were clammy, my knees like water. I didn't want my seven-year-old daughter to know how I was feeling, or the Archbishop's wife, or anyone for that matter. It was David's day and I had no wish to draw attention to myself. I saw everything through a confusing mist of excitement and terror. I was excited by the party atmosphere, and terrified by the awesome responsibility which I would share with David. I wondered what would be expected of me, and whether I would meet these expectations. I felt unsafe in the front row. But I survived, and I doubt whether anyone noticed my acute anxiety. I had put on a good show, and kidded everyone – but not myself. Like the swan gliding up river, I was cool, calm, and collected on the surface, and paddling like mad underneath.

From that day there began a completely new life of learning how to confront my feelings of isolation, and to balance the private with the public. I had realised that David would be out most days, fulfilling demanding engagements around his half of the Southwark Diocese. Jenny and I had to make a life of our own. As she was at primary school, I found the quiet very strange. No one came to my door as they used to. I was in a new neighbourhood, four miles from my friends across the water at the Mayflower. So I had to go out to meet my neighbours, and the wider community, myself. This was a daunting prospect, which I realised could only be tackled by me. So one day I opened my front door and began to brush the steps. It was the best I could do. I felt very unsure of myself, but I was determined not to give up. I had to begin somewhere. And so from this beginning sprang a stream of conversations and contacts with passers-by and local residents, from pensioners to groups of black school children. They became friends.

Quite soon it was clear that we had come to stay and I was asked to join a number of organisations. I became a governor of the comprehensive school opposite our front door, a member of the Parochial Church Council of St John's, Peckham, our local parish church, and a member of the Clifton Crescent Action Group, fighting to save a set of listed buildings from demolition, for the benefit of local residents. I opened a Christmas Market locally, and accepted my first solo engagement further afield up the Old Kent Road. To each of these events I travelled by car even though most were walking distance – I was too frightened to walk. Once there, I had no problem in taking a full and active part. Very few people were aware that I was afraid of anything.

During the next six years I combined several tasks. As well as providing a home for David and Jenny there was a lovely, well stocked garden to be kept in order. We also decided to entertain on a regular basis. These parties were among my happiest experiences. We would invite, at regular intervals, a mixed group of clergy and others – about fifteen at a time – to an informal fork supper. I would cater for it all and Jenny and David would be valiant helpers. I had put to good use the Mayflower years of relative confinement by teaching myself to cook.

Meanwhile, there were new challenges outside the home. I had to learn to attend big services, dress up for formal dinners, and to attend grand civic occasions, including visits to Buckingham Palace and the Mansion House. I had a further duty. As our diocesan bishop, Mervyn Stockwood, was unmarried, there arose the question of the pastoral care of clergy wives. For a short while I was the only bishop's wife in the Southwark Diocese. Much was expected of me, and I found this daunting. Neither Mervyn Stockwood nor David put pressure on me, but I knew I had to do something. David and I visited the homes of the 150 clergy in his half of the Diocese during our first year. We loved this and know it was appreciated. I greatly enjoyed calling on the wives of the clergy, even babysitting for them occasionally.

I was greatly relieved when Eliza Montefiore, wife of the new Bishop of Kingston, arrived. Together we organised evenings in the Cathedral Chapter House, with a meal and entertainment; Donald Swann was a great favourite. As the more 'senior' bishop's wife, it was agreed that I would take charge. I was very nervous and dreaded those evenings, but I struggled through – though I needed the next day in which to recover.

Because David's diary was so full, I would sometimes venture out alone to the deanery parties for clergy couples which were a feature of the Southwark Diocese – and would enjoy them. It was easier for me to travel by night; I felt freer and more relaxed when darkness fell, and less exposed. But I was not able to avoid exposure for long.

In 1974 speculation began over who should succeed Stuart Blanch as Bishop of Liverpool. Having assisted Mervyn Stockwood, as Bishop of Woolwich, for six years, David's name was being mentioned as a likely choice. (Ladbrokes even opened a book on the subject, offering tips.) We were staying with David's mother when, on the 3rd January 1975, the telephone rang. It was David's secretary. Over the 'phone she read the invitation from the Prime Minister to David to be the next Bishop of Liverpool. David's mother, who dreaded his moving north and further away from her, collapsed into tears, and so did I. My tears were a mixture of empathy with her and relief that the time of speculation was now over. David set himself to deciding.

In three days the letter of acceptance was in the post. David's mother and sister were remarkably accepting and supportive. So were my parents. We were off on another adventure, and a radical change was in store.

Selling our home in Peckham was a great wrench, and leaving our friends was as difficult. But we arrived at Lime Street station in Liverpool eagerly peering out of the train window. I was looking forward to seeing the house, though I was dismayed when I found it was some distance from the city centre – a new journey for me to master.

We visited the Cathedral on the Sunday morning. Jenny, now thirteen years old, was with us. As we entered the vast building, built with huge blocks of pink sandstone, I was struck with how few people were there, and how small we all seemed. It was extremely cold; it was Lent, so there were no flowers. No other children were present. I was filled with a sense of foreboding. This was going to be 'our' cathedral, the place where so many – mistakenly – assume the bishop lives by night and by day; our home in Woolton would be twenty minutes away by car. Feelings of confusion overwhelmed me. Mercifully the figure of the Dean, Edward Patey, tall and slightly dishevelled, appeared; he greeted us discreetly and warmly. He and Maggie, his wife, were to become firm and trusted friends and colleagues.

But despite the welcome I was becoming increasingly uneasy. I couldn't see the warmth in the cathedral's pink sandstone. It looked blue to me. I had become used to South-wark Cathedral, which was relatively intimate and informal, and was usually quite full. The music for which Liverpool Cathedral was famed was solemn and seemed miles away. A huge wave of loneliness came over me and I was afraid.

25

I was miserable and determined not to show it. But this determination came very close to masquerading and hypocrisy, and hypocrisy was something that Jesus could not tolerate, especially in people of influence. This would surely include church leaders – and I imagined that applied to their wives as well.

Underlying all these disabling feelings was a bigger one. I had come to acknowledge the fact of my phobia of public open spaces, and this massive cathedral was one hell of an open space. Many questions called for an answer. Where would 'they' want me to sit? Would it be the front row? I thought I would suffocate with dread. Pretending that I was happy to sit in an honoured place presented huge problems, and I felt powerless. Bishops' wives do not and must not rock the boat, I told myself, especially when they have just arrived. It would complicate things for my husband, who had enough on his mind. 'Don't make a fuss', I thought. In protecting everyone else I left myself exposed, and battled on.

So during the next seven years I sat in my appointed place at every service, pinching myself till it hurt under my purpose-bought cloak of warm green woollen cloth. The pinching helped divert my attention from the feelings of panic that would arise, most often during the sermon or gospel reading when everyone was still and had no books to fiddle with. The cloak would ensure that no one noticed. Underneath there was a struggling human being desperately pretending to look at ease.

My problem was not a total secret. I had shared it with members of my family and close friends. I sensed their loving acceptance, which spurred me on to want to find ways of conquering the power of these destructive feelings. I had been urged by an older colleague to share my difficulties more widely in the diocese if I felt able. 'It would help people to understand when you refuse to speak at meetings,' she said. But I was unsure how to set about it.

Shortly after arriving in Liverpool, David was invited to take part in a television programme, 'Anno Domini'. It was an attempt to examine, as truthfully as possible, the story behind the 'success' figure. He invited me to join him. So after much careful thought and discussion with the producer, Bill Nicholson, we decided that, if I could muster the courage, I should talk about my experience of fear and agoraphobia. After all, it had been a shared experience, and was certainly part of David's life. We felt we had positive things to say, and so did Bill. Thanks to his extreme care and understanding the programme went out on the air, uncut. It was risky; I was fearful of being labelled 'neurotic', 'poor little thing', 'delicate' and 'invalid' – all names I had studied to avoid. However, I did want to own the label, 'human being', knowing it to be true.

None of us was prepared for the reaction of the viewing public. We received over a thousand letters from people all over the country, both men and women, and to this day, over thirteen years later, each of us independently is still approached by people saying how much the programme helped them or a friend. 'If a bishop's wife can feel like that, then I do not feel so alone. It makes me feel more ordinary and less of a freak. I feel released.'

Taking part in that programme made us feel that we were part of a releasing action, and something creative. The opportunity to share so publicly was costly, but it also saved us from having to live a private secret within a public life. It was an invitation to tell the truth and to share a little more of our humanity.

Sharing my experience like this was not only releasing for others, it was therapeutic for me, but I needed adequate support. The companionship, love and trust of my husband, together with the integrity and skill of the producer and his team, provided security. It helped me to find the courage to risk my reputation in this way. I believe that that is Christ's way; we don't have to be public people to learn how to be honest, to share, to take courage, and risk facing fear together. But we do need to be there for one another. 'Love one another as I have loved you', begins to hold exciting new meaning. God comes near to us in one another. We can begin to discover how to give life to each other, releasing the grip of fear. We can find fear giving way to love.

But during the next few years, there came increasing pressures, and I felt the need to confront my fears. I was exhausted with keeping up appearances. I decided to consult a therapist.

My sessions with a clinical psychologist were both illuminating and liberating. Sometimes they were painful. The psychologist encouraged me to talk about my fears, and I decided to trust her with them. She helped me to understand that I had the power to make decisions concerning my own life, and needed to exercise it. Her absolute and steady acceptance of me, fears, confusions and guilts, was a revelation. Gradually I learned to accept myself. I felt she was exhibiting God's love as he meant it to be. I did not feel judged by her, yet learned how harshly I had been judging myself and others. I came to see that the key to freedom lay in my own hands, and that I would have to work for this freedom. She supported me faithfully when facing painful situations, without doing the work for me. I began to feel more ordinary, less of an oddity, and more comfortable with my fears, amazed at how they could dissolve when firmly confronted. At the same time, I began to feel more special, and unafraid to be what I am, which is a vulnerable human being, yet made in the image of God, capable of making good things happen.

As well as this kind of support, I sought out a spiritual director who could be there to guide me while I was learning to control my fears. I wanted him to help me identify God in the tougher times as well as when the going was easier. He had a sense of humour and helped me to laugh at myself. He also managed to convey that he too was a vulnerable human being under God, unwilling to patronise or judge. Both my counsellors did not cling on to their professionalism to elicit my trust, but offered their skills and their time, leaving me space to grow in confidence at my own pace. I felt they trusted me. I felt respected. They maintained the distance of good professionals, yet offered the closeness of friends; I felt they enjoyed my company. That gave me a sense of worth.

Building on the love and acceptance of my husband, family and friends, I began not only to accept myself, but also to sense the life-giving love of God. I breathed a new atmosphere of acceptance and grace, where I was free from constant and pressurising judgement. God became again the God of love and tenderness I had known as a child. He offered freedom and wholeness, provided I was honest about my fears, and was prepared to accept them as part of the humanness of me. The grip of fear began to loosen, and new confidence began to flow. I had begun to take charge of my life.

4

Acknowledging Fear

One of the great lessons I learned as I progressed towards self-confidence is that it is human to be afraid, and nothing to feel guilty about. It has nothing to do with sin, or with doing wrong. Fear is a feeling, and a sign that we are alive. Without it we are probably suffering from a physical or mental handicap. It is a signal that danger is near. We need to feel fear.

So it is vital that we acknowledge that signal and discover what it is communicating to us. The red flag on the beach is a sign that it is dangerous to swim. If we were to disregard the flag, or decide that it was not important, we would be asking for trouble. Not to acknowledge fear in ourselves is rather like disregarding the red flag on the beach, and just as dangerous.

My story is only one of millions. Yet some fears are easier to own than others. It is not difficult to acknowledge being afraid in a general sense, and neither do we mind owning fears that others talk about more openly. Most of us would be quite ready to say we are terrified of being squeezed to death by a boa-constrictor. This can be regarded as a respectable fear, for we do not lose respect by admitting it. But admitting to being afraid of crossing a road feels far more dangerous, and is far less respectable. So we keep it to ourselves, hoping that no one else will notice. It will help us, if we can stop and notice that we *are* afraid.

Acknowledging or noticing is the first important step to the effective management of fear. We need to build a relationship with our feeling of fear just as if we were in charge of any army of soldiers, or a large class of lively children. The soldiers, and the pupils, need to be noticed. Our fears are like that, and need acknowledging in the same way. They belong to us, and need to be welcomed as such.

Acknowledging is simple. Think of two drivers. Driving along a narrow country lane we may meet a car coming in the opposite direction. Many lanes have passing places, and when two drivers arrive at a passing place, they slow down and acknowledge each other by raising a hand, sometimes with a smile. We need to slow down, and acknowledge fear like that.

If we refuse to notice fears, we begin to allow them to dictate how we behave. We will not be in control, but will instead be possessed and driven by our fears. This will lead us to become confused and divided inside, and go on to produce forms of anger and violence. Take, for example, a man who has been afraid all his life of being left behind, and now he is afraid that his wife is overtaking him intellectually. Rather than acknowledge his fear of being left behind, he begins to be angry with her, blaming her for neglecting the family, and for other difficulties in their marriage. He becomes jealous of her achievements, and behaves in a way that is destructive to her, to himself and to their relationship. He begins to compare himself with her unfavourably, putting himself down, and so does emotional violence to himself as well as to her. This can also lead to physical violence. Because he does not acknowledge his initial fear, he begins to lose control, and that sets up a cycle of behaviour which leads to panic. He needs to slow down, notice his deeper fear, and decide early what he wants to do with this feeling, if he can, before it begins to drive him.

Unacknowledged fear is dangerous and, like nuclear waste, it cannot be disposed of; it can only be stored. In many ways unacknowledged fear is more powerful than nuclear waste, because it cannot be stored safely away. It goes on acting and developing in destructive ways. Bottle it up, and we have the beginnings of anger and violence. Angry people are often fearful people who are afraid of losing their ground.

Destruction or violence is generally the last resort before

31

giving up altogether. Violent people have given up hope of surviving in any other way.

Facing fears means facing facts, and facing the truth can be uncomfortable, but it does slowly release the grip of fear, bringing life. We need to face the truth because it stops us from pretending. It helps us to avoid deceiving ourselves, and deceiving other people. It helps us to be more fully human, and more able to enjoy the gift of life in company with others. But we may need to pause and reassess our picture of the perfect human being, and discover what we are aiming for.

Our stereotyped image of the perfectly developed, balanced person does not at first sight include someone who has much feeling. We form these pictures during our adolescent years. Pop idols, the perfect mother, footballer or model are usually from a world removed from our own. They are often figures who have achieved some measure of success in their own fields, uncluttered by tears or wrinkles or anything that would suggest that they would bleed if punctured with a pin. They become our idols or saints with halos, people to worship and emulate. So for Christians to have presented to them, as their image of perfection, someone who was disfigured and hurt, someone who suffered at the hands of his fellow human beings, raises a problem. Which figure do we really want? We need to decide what we regard as truly human, and put away all false images. It is unhelpful to stay with the idols of our adolescence if they appear in pictures to be perfectly controlled, tidy, successful and uncomplicated people. The truth behind the image is likely to be both more interesting and more disturbing, and infinitely more exciting. Most of all it will be human.

Despite the fact that we have a suffering vulnerable figure as our God, we Christians still have so much to learn. We still project an image of people whose experience is removed from that of those outside the church. I learned this from a docker and his wife who started to come to our church in east London. A church member lost his temper in front of our visitors, and there was a row. Immediately the docker expressed his surprise and relief that these Christians were human too, and decided to continue coming to church.

The sanitised, Persil-white Christian is disturbing to many on the fringes of the church, because they know that people like that are too good to be true. Church should be a place where we can be truly ourselves, accepted as we are, and not a place where we pretend.

It is important to learn to be more honest, because that frees us from living a split life, thinking one thing and doing another, such as pretending that we are unafraid when inside we are quaking. Sometimes we *have* to act like this but we must, at least privately, acknowledge how we feel. Acknowledging fear like this helps us live more honestly with other people, recognising that they too share similar feelings from time to time.

As well as bringing freedom, being more honest with ourselves and with each other can be fun.

I experienced this one day when David had been delayed, and so I was putting the finishing touches to a meal for fifteen people and welcoming the guests at the same time. It became very busy, and the room was filling up unusually quickly. When David arrived home, he took one look at the room and whispered in my ear, 'We've got next week's as well!' True enough, I must have sent out the invitations with the same date to two sets of people. So that meant fifteen extra to cater for. Anxious that there would not be enough food, but also keen to impress my guests, I began to wonder whether to pretend that nothing had happened.

On reflection, I decided that as I was the one responsible, I would own up to what had happened. As soon as they heard, our guests, who had been on their best behaviour, became more relaxed. They laughed, offered sympathy, and practical help. Half an hour later, the party was humming with life. I felt free from anxiety, and our guests were freed from their roles. We became human together, and created a new and lively experience.

But often we are reluctant to be as honest, because fear drives us to believe that we will be rejected, that we are in some way guilty of something. This rejection feels like the final judgement. So in order to avoid even thinking about that, we stifle our fear – and press on. When we do this we shut off part of who we are, or divide ourselves into parts that we can accept and parts that we cannot. We don't want to be judged for what we feel, but for what we do. Because we are so afraid of making mistakes, of getting it wrong, and of failing, we shut off the more disturbing feelings and refuse to acknowledge their presence – which makes them all the more frightening.

Many of us have spent years dodging from the truth about how we feel, afraid that to acknowledge fear to ourselves would be an admission of sin and failure. But fear is not a sin. It is not failure. It is simply a sign that we are alive. So we need to look at it as squarely as we are able, and find ways of welcoming these disturbing feelings, acknowledging them as part of our vital equipment for a life of loving.

As well as noticing our fears in a general sense, we need to be specific. Just as the teacher will try to know each individual pupil, so we need to acknowledge our fears as they appear. They belong to us, and we need to own each of them.

Acknowledging a specific fear helps us to be clear what we are fighting, and where the danger actually lies. It prevents us from being caught up in a world of unreality. A general fear which is difficult to put into words can set the whole alarm system going. It is worth making the time to try to put into words what we are actually feeling, by talking to a trusted person or expressing our feelings on paper. In that way we can isolate our fears before they isolate us, making them easier to control.

I have kept a diary for some years. Occasionally, I have written down what I fear about some future event. One entry reads like this:

Monday, October 12th, 4.30 p.m.
Today I visited H, and shared my great dread of Thursday (Centenary Celebrations in the Cathedral) with her. My ticket is labelled No.1. That means a seat in the front row. Very Important! No escaping that that is where I am expected to sit. How can I handle this great fear?

Then I listed some of the factors to face:

> I don't want to sit in the front row.
> I must.
> I will.
> Find a way of living inside the trap.
> There is no such thing as life without fear. We all have it.
> I can expect this phobia to ease. But I cannot expect fear
> to disappear.

Later, in a letter to my mother, I wrote,

> I managed to sit in Seat No. 1 in the front row, throughout.
> It wasn't easy, but with careful preparation I made it . . .
> I'd decided to look for signs of human life from within my
> 'trap' and found lots. They ranged from a 'Gosh-fancy-
> sitting-there' grin from Mark, to the clergy procession
> beginning to go haywire as they ran to keep up, robes flying
> and with grinning faces . . .

It helped me to write the facts down. The problem did not
disappear, but became more manageable, and afterwards
I had a sense of achievement that I had managed my
fear.

This is one of my own ways of dealing with fear. But we
have to recognise that communities, as well as individuals,
can allow fear to grow out of all proportion. We have to deal
with – and help – the fear of others. I have seen this most
movingly done in a potentially dangerous situation.

Some years ago, I attended a service in the Liverpool parish
church. The Archbishop of Canterbury, Robert Runcie, was
to be the preacher; it was immediately before the Pope's visit
to the city in 1982. High feelings were running against the
visit among members of the Orange Lodge; many of them
had come to this service to protest against the Archbishop's
lead towards closer ties between the Anglican and Catholic
Churches. The church was packed. Half of it was filled with
screaming, shouting people, some of them standing on the
pews while the Archbishop tried to deliver his address. Sens-

ing that he was not to be allowed a hearing, he turned and knelt at the altar in prayer for some time. Then, rising to his feet, he slowly walked toward the door of the church and stopped very close to where I was sitting. A woman was shouting abuse as he passed. He turned to her and said, 'Don't be afraid. There's nothing to be afraid of.' In the heart of the storm, he had found something peaceful to say. He did not blame or judge, but simply acknowledged her fear, and that of her friends, and she stopped shouting.

These people were afraid that ecumenical relations would lead to Protestant churches being swallowed up by Rome under the control of the Pope. Their fear had turned to uncontrollable anger, which threatened to terminate any rational relationship. But once one of that group realised that someone was listening, and taking notice, she became less angry and more able to understand that her life was not in danger. She had less need to shout. Acknowledging her fear diffused her anger.

As well as being more definite, we need this openness, this understanding of others, if we are to free ourselves – and each other – from fear.

We need to be more truthful. It is hard to face the truth about ourselves because so much of it is hidden away. We hide, both from ourselves, and from each other, out of fear. Occasionally we will meet someone who is able to show his or her humanity a little more truthfully, and that bit of truth frees others to be human too.

There is room for more openness, and less inhibition, in our behaviour. There is room for more passion. We will become more credible human beings, and more truthful people, if we can be ourselves more fully. Our families know the truth about us. They see the swings of mood and strength of feeling. If we are honest, we see these too. It is unmanaged fear that drives us to pretend. It is this fear that prevents us from letting go a little more.

Acknowledging our real selves, and acknowledging our fear, becomes easier when we accept that there is a child in us still, learning how to handle the natural responses that have been implanted to keep us alive, healthy and safe. Growing children are, by nature, dependent on parents or guardians. These are the people who, ideally, first give children a feeling that they are safe from harm.

But real life can be rough on children. They get hurt, both physically and emotionally. Grandparents die, parents leave or divorce, guardians change and schools get closed. Children experience bereavement and loss, and feelings of fear take root. Their alarm systems begin to form, and the alarm bells of our youth go on ringing in later life; it helps to acknowledge that, as part of who we are.

For example, I have a fear of being left to cope alone. This fear developed during the Second World War when the doodlebugs were flying over, pilotless and threatening. As an evacuated nine-year-old, I remember wondering, with acute anxiety, whether one would fall on us at school, or on my mother, my young brother, and our new baby at home. The threat of being blown up and separated, was real. That memory is part of me. I am not ashamed of the feeling it leaves me with, and it does not make me less responsible now. But when I feel that fear reverberating again, I need to acknowledge that it is there, and then to decide how to deal with it.

Decision is an adult privilege. As adults we are faced with choices, for we have some power and control over the way we behave. If we leave decisions to others we are not taking responsibility for ourselves; we will remain undeveloped and stunted emotionally.

When faced with feelings of fear, we need to decide what to do with those feelings in order to manage them before they take charge and dictate our behaviour, driving us to destructive actions like nagging or lying. We can, for instance, decide to face fear alone, or in the company of others. As children, it was unusual to face fear alone. If we felt like talking there was someone else with whom to share our feelings – a grandmother, parent or teacher. They would listen and guide us, helping us to handle the fear. It was natural for us to share and natural to acknowledge how frightened we were. As we grew older this became harder.

None of us has completely grown up. No one can claim to have finished their development until they die. So we need to accept ourselves as we are, acknowledging the natural God-given responses, including fear.

But acknowledging fear is not easy at first, particularly if we condemn it in others or regard it as a sign of failure in ourselves. We hear voices saying, 'Big boys do not cry', and 'Christians should not be afraid'. In our youth we have received this impression, and we have grown up to believe it is true.

Big boys do cry, and Christians are afraid, but it does not end there. In our longing to be whole, integrated people, we can have misconceptions of what we mean by whole, inte-grated and mature. We have come to believe that to be completely adult or grown up, is to be self-sufficient, indepen-dent and reliable. Most of us want to be like that. Yet the ideal we see, on the one hand, is someone who is so complete that he has nothing to receive, is so whole that there is nothing left to mend, and is so adult that the responses of a child have long since gone.

But there is another ideal. Jesus, the perfectly mature human being, shows us a man who cried, and a person who was afraid. Here we can see the child in the man, the whole and human expression of what it means to grow. Not to acknowledge the child in ourselves is to shut our eyes to the truth, and only facing the truth will make us whole. This wholeness is reflected in people who take time to play, to express fear and joy in unaffected responses, and who are not too stiff or proud to depend from time to time on others, receiving help and forgiveness.

Much suffering can be caused by believing that Christians should not be afraid. Christians are afraid, and so they should be. It is nothing to feel guilty about, but rather to be thankful for, as their feelings of fear, like everyone else's, are signs of being alive. It is often suggested in Christian circles that, because of the presence of Christ, they are never alone, and so never need to feel afraid. This only means something when we understand that Christ's presence is there in one another as well as in each individual who acknowledges him. If we can accept that, then we will begin to understand how to acknowledge him, by accepting each other as part of a great whole, and believing that each person has the potential for loving and healing. Each of us who wants the Spirit of Christ to be active in him or herself needs to find ways of accepting Christ as fully human, acknowledging his feelings of fear as well as our own. If Christ shed tears and also knew fear, then that is an overwhelming reason to believe that it is all right for Christians to do the same. Christians need not feel ashamed or guilty for feeling afraid; we are simply being human, like the founder of our faith.

5

Sharing Fear

Acknowledging our fears becomes easier when we begin to realise what we have in common with other people. When we begin to realise that fear is part of being human, we experience a new freedom. Keeping up the pretence of being free from fear is exhausting and inwardly painful. It is like being caught up in a thicket of sharp thorns, and at the same time pretending that all is well. But some people have been in the thicket for a long time, and the disentangling will be slow.

Living in the grip of fears can make us feel very alone, and that there is no one else who understands our difficulty. We are tempted to give up the struggle, allowing the fears to tighten their grip all the more. But it is never too late to begin discovering new freedom, and sharing can help.

After the TV programme in which I took part, it became much more generally known that even a bishop's wife could suffer quite disabling fear. As a result, my hairdresser told me of a woman related to one of her clients who had suffered from agoraphobia for over twenty years, and had not told anyone beyond her doctor and close family. My hairdresser wondered if I could help. As soon as the woman plucked up courage to contact me direct, I went straight to her home. I found her agitated and apologetic, but willing to talk. We talked together about how she was feeling, and about my experience of knowing the terror of leaving the safety of my home. She told me that she had no interest in anything, and that for some time she had stopped cleaning the house, leaving that to her daughter and husband. She said she felt ashamed for being as she was, crippled with fear and unable to go out alone.

As we talked, I could see a lively, fun-loving, creative person trapped by fear. Her body was tense, but inside, her eyes were dancing. Quite soon she began to brighten, and said she did not feel nearly so bad now that she had seen, with her own eyes, someone who understood. She felt comforted to meet someone who had shared something of the same experience, and who no longer felt trapped by it. She felt less alone.

Some weeks later I returned, and no sooner had I rung the bell, than her husband opened the door and shook my hand vigorously. He said, 'I don't know what you have done; she's a changed woman.' Astonished, I walked in to find her sitting once more on her sofa, but this time smiling shyly. On the floor in front of her was a pile of blue knitting. 'What's that?' I asked. 'It's a jumper for my daughter,' she said, 'I've never done any knitting before. And I cleaned all the crockery this morning.'

There is in most of us a deep need to share. But not everyone can find a friend nearby. Telephone listening services, like the Samaritans and other more local organisations, are overwhelmed with calls. Aircare, to which viewers of some religious TV programmes are invited to ring in if they need help, is inundated with calls.

These services reveal a deep and terrible loneliness among the many who genuinely have no one to care about them: the widowed; the elderly; young mothers, perhaps single, trapped in high-rise blocks; and the many, particularly in the centres of large cities and on outer estates, who have lost any feeling of being part of a family or of a community. Loneliness like this makes us feel dry and shut in on ourselves, unable to change our situation. We become depressed. Breaking the cycle of this kind of loneliness is hard, especially for those unable to travel, or who have no telephone, or do not know any of the people living nearby.

There is another, deeper kind of loneliness, a loneliness that is different from being alone. We can feel lonely in a crowd, and unable to reach or be reached by another person.

41

Feeling lonely then means that, despite the fact that we have family, friends and neighbours to turn to, we find ourselves unable to approach them. It also means that when we do identify someone we would like to talk to, something prevents us from approaching them, and we begin to make excuses. We think they are too busy and will not want to be bothered with us and our troubles. So we shut ourselves away from sharing with anyone, afraid of further hurt. Withdrawing like this is different from just being alone.

To be alone is something we can choose freely. We all need some time and space to ourselves, some more than others. Too much isolation, however, is unhealthy. We need to find a balance.

Finding the balance takes time, but there are ways in which we can help ourselves to feel less lonely. Someone I know sent out several postcards of greetings to different people when she felt depressed. This action produced responses that made her feel less lonely, and her friends in turn were glad to be remembered. Others of us may choose to go for a walk in the park, wander into a church or cathedral, or take a bus ride. We can make the effort to contact a close friend before allowing the reasons against to take over. Having identified the loneliness, it is important to share it early, before it becomes deeper and more difficult to dispel.

A friend of ours was once faced with a difficult family problem which threatened to isolate her. As it was of a sensitive nature, it was not easy to share many of her feelings with those closer to her. So she wrote an account of what happened on one sheet of paper, and sent it to us to read. At the end of her story she wrote, 'Thank you for listening. I feel much better now that I have shared this.' She set herself free from being enclosed with her fears, which would have allowed them more opportunity to drive her further into a destructive isolation.

It would have been helpful if I had learned to share more easily when I was new to Liverpool. As a bishop's wife, I felt that people had expectations of me. One day one of these included providing tea and cakes for a group of sixty people. I had become physically tired with the preparations, and to make matters worse, David was in bed with 'flu'. Our local vicar came to visit. After chatting for a while, he turned to me and asked, 'And how are you?' I was so surprised to receive this attention, that I didn't collect myself in time and dissolved into tears. I told him that I was completely exhausted. While there was certainly some self-pity in my complaints, I was principally feeling very lonely, not knowing who to turn to, or how to ask for help. Although there were hundreds of willing helpers within reach among the parishes, I thought everyone else was too busy, and so I battled on alone. Until that moment I could not even admit to myself that I was lonely. After all, I thought stiffly, bishops' wives are grown-up people, and ought to be able to cope with problems. I rushed to judge myself for not being grown-up, for not 'coping'.

This judgement was prompted by a host of other fears which began to take control: fear of failing people's expectations; fear of losing my dignity by admitting I needed help; fear of losing enthusiasm for a new job by the prospect of more exhaustion; fear of criticism and disapproval if I said 'No' next time; and of losing my reputation for being a supportive wife. The list was a long one.

The vicar's simple question, 'How are you?' unlocked my imprisoned spirit. I felt released, and in acknowledging my true feelings, I was able to find new energy. There are simple questions which we can ask one another. 'What's the matter?' 'How are you?' But they must be asked with sincerity, and answered with honesty. We can always ask ourselves these questions first, identifying how we are feeling and acknowledging our fears privately.

Acknowledging and facing our fears privately is the first step towards wholeness. But to stop there can lead to a special kind of loneliness, the loneliness that springs from the idea that we can be totally self-sufficient.

Deeply rooted in our society there is a belief that it is better for us to be independent, coping individuals, and that to ask for help is weak. This belief springs from a fear of over-involvement with each other, and a fear of being overwhelmed by another's power. We are afraid of losing control. Our fear of over-involvement turns imperceptibly into the fear of any involvement, and we begin to isolate ourselves from one another. We search feverishly for what we feel will be a safe place, so that we can survive. We take steps to detach or isolate ourselves because we are afraid, and begin to call that isolation 'independence'. We develop an island mentality, surrounding ourselves with a sea of loneliness. Not wanting to appear dependent, we put up a façade of independence until we believe our own pretence. Because of our pride, we begin to believe that we are self-sufficient, and become increasingly unable to acknowledge what we can and do receive from others.

This self-inflicted isolation gradually causes us to appear aloof or shy, and we put out messages that we do not want to be approached at all, and so increase our own loneliness and fear of losing control. We find it increasingly difficult to entrust ourselves to another person in friendship, believing that we are being more mature by coping independently. Underneath, though, we remain ill at ease, and long to find our way back to the place where once we were more carefree.

Sharing our fears with anyone is risky. It feels dangerous. We risk losing control, losing our reputation and our dignity. We also risk rejection; our listener may judge us and desert us. This feeling leads to a dread of being cut off and excluded. But this need not be so. It takes determination to look out for someone to trust, and then courage to ask him or her to listen.

For many people, being brought up in a large and loving family has meant a greater chance of learning about trusting relationships. Others will have found that, in both large and small families, they were let down, deserted, or felt betrayed once too often to risk trusting anyone again. Death, divorce and separation have shaken the foundations of many homes and left the children with experiences of hurt and bitterness which remain life-long memories. For most of us, betrayal early in life, or an experience of being overwhelmed, hurts, and we begin to put up barriers against it happening again. As we become older, it will be that much harder to face the world at large, if we have not learned to bridge our feelings of loneliness by making our own friends. Eventually, the death of a partner may feel like a betrayal of trust, as the loss is a great one, and we will need other trusted friends with whom to share our grief.

Friendship is vital. So much of today's advertising and fiction focuses on romantic love, that we have forgotten how important friendship is. Not only can friendship be the answer to loneliness, it can also provide the basis for creating a place where we can help each other to flourish and grow. It is not hard to understand why Christ used this image to describe the relationship he wanted us to experience with him. He said, 'I have called you friends.'

Friendship can be enjoyed on different levels, and making friends with someone involves trusting them and being trusted by them. It is a two-way process. We need to feel safe if we are to entrust ourselves at all deeply to one another.

Making friends is a costly and risky business, but infinitely rewarding. But we are often in such a hurry, that we don't give ourselves time to think about, or practise, making good friendships that will last. Then we wonder why we feel lonely, cut-off, and unable to share both our fears and our joys. The old song, 'Everybody needs somebody sometime', is true. I would go further; everybody needs somebody always. To know that a friend whom we can trust is at hand, is a vital ingredient for healthy living.

We need to choose our friends carefully. There are people who appear to find it easy to talk to anyone about their fears. Being unselective in this way has peculiar problems. It means that a potentially close relationship is invited with every encounter, and expectations are raised which cannot be realised. This reaching out for 'instant friends' suggests that a person is unable to choose someone to trust, and so shares indiscriminately, hoping that in each relationship something will emerge to make them feel less lonely or fearful. Such behaviour suggests a lostness and hopelessness that comes from much deeper problems.

Being a growing person involves making choices, and that includes choosing whom we confide in, and how many we trust in this way. Consulting too many people creates confusion, and can be as unhelpful as not sharing with anyone. As there are many different levels of fear, so there are different levels of relationship; some will be deeper than others. We need to distinguish the levels, and to maintain our side of any relationship we choose to make. Finding a friend to trust, and who entrusts themselves to us is finding something very valuable, and is to be treasured. Sharing our fears in this way is both healing and life-giving. We shall not discover this treasure unless we are prepared to take some risks.

Making friends is an adventure, and takes courage. It is dangerous because it involves trust, openness and love, and if trust is betrayed, then openness turns to cynicism, and love can turn into hatred and rejection. The fear of betrayal, cynicism and rejection often prevents us from even attempting the art of friendship. So we allow ourselves to be caught in a cycle of fear. But this way we deny ourselves one of the most creative pursuits in the world. In effect, we create our own isolation and deny any possibility of being comforted, healed or helped by a friend. We also deny ourselves the friendship that Christ invited us to share with himself. How can we contemplate that invitation without at least trying to experience friendship with our fellow human beings? It is an adventure worth trying.

Sharing our fears involves trust. If we have not yet managed to make good trusting friendships, or if our fears have grown to such proportions that they are too private or disturbing to entrust even to a close friend, then there are other possibilities. There are growing numbers of trained counsellors, spiritual directors and therapists, who know how to stand by a person who feels gripped or paralysed by their own fears. If we choose to consult a professional counsellor, or a clergyman, it is likely that our fears are driving us hard, but not so hard that we cannot shout for help. It will be a sign that we are still managing our lives, even if it does not feel like it at the time.

There are skilled social workers and organisations, where those with problems can go, knowing that they will not be judged or punished. There are many ordained men and women in the Church who know how to keep a confidence,

46

and who would be glad to be asked to help. If they are good professionals, they will also know how to acknowledge their own fears privately, to themselves, and will not be too proud to have sought help from someone else.

Many lay people, both men and women, sign up for some of the excellent counselling courses available in order to equip themselves with skills in listening, and with knowledge which enables them to notice when they are getting out of their depth. This training is valuable, and gives confidence to those who want to help in this way, but who also know they have a lot to learn.

There are others who, discovering their interest in counselling and other areas of therapy or healing, go on to study more deeply, and become professional psychiatrists, psychologists and psychotherapists. Clergy too receive training in caring for people, and some go on to build on that training, knowing that they need to learn how to listen, as do social workers and others in the caring professions.

It is possible to share our fears with a professional person who has been properly trained. We need the wisdom of others, just as they need the knowledge that fresh experience brings. Good training builds in adequate supervision. Without it, professional arrogance can thrive until a person believes he or she has all the answers and is unable to take advice from anyone.

Consulting a trained professional is no more dangerous than making any other relationship. It feels risky because we cannot know in advance what will happen when we begin to entrust ourselves to another person. In fact we are taking responsibility for how we feel. Choosing to talk to someone when we need help is healthy, especially if we don't abandon responsibility; we can decide what to talk about, and when to stop. The counsellor is there to share in the healing process, and not to produce a magic solution.

My experience with a professional therapist has been most liberating. Finding that I was totally accepted, and learning to accept myself in the same way, with all my crippling fears, has done a great deal to help me rediscover my original self-confidence. It has also illuminated the kind of relationship that Christ came to show us. To have someone sensitively 'alongside' while I groped my own way back to firmer ground, interpreting, encouraging, believing in my ability to manage, has been most rewarding. I have been fortunate to have that image of Christ reinforced by my husband, friends and family. But my fears had been allowed to get a grip for too long, until they ruled, so consulting a professional took some of the strain off my family. There are limits sometimes to what we ask of those closest to us, however patient they may be.

One of the best places however to learn about acceptance, is in a marriage partnership. Here there is mutual commitment and, above all, ideally, mutual love. The potential for deep friendship and honest, responsible living is infinite. Because we are prepared to give so much in marriage, we also expect a great deal. Accepting each other's humanity is an important prerequisite for a good marriage. Accepting each other's ability to feel fear is another.

At home and in the marriage relationship, it is more difficult to pretend. We live, eat and sleep together. At home, we feel freer to say and do what we feel like than we do outside. But with this freedom comes the responsibility to love and to care with more than just words. Taking each other for granted is something we should rightly fear. Any loving relationship involves effort and real work to maintain it. Part of the work is to take time and trouble to be together, discovering one another's needs, and enjoying one another's company. As soon as one partner begins to feel either crowded or deserted by the other, then it is wise to say so, so that a balance can be worked for. Once fears are allowed to control our actions, then we begin to become defensive and love is given no room to thrive. Our natural responses need to be recognised. Love accepts, so that we have no need to pretend.

Some people who come for professional help, could be helped earlier if as a society we were more open with each other, and more accepting. There are many fears that assume huge proportions and prevent the sufferers from feeling able to talk about them with anyone. For example, a mother with post-natal depression can't share her experience with anyone – she is afraid of losing face, and her fear drives her to hide her true feelings until she snaps. Or there is a father who is afraid of relating to his adolescent child, and his fear of failure and rejection drives him to give his child surrogate and expensive gifts he can ill afford. A student arrives at college, and joins a group of apparently like-minded people. After a while he finds that they have a set of values which he cannot share. Fear of being rejected or laughed at, if he shares his problem, drives him to avoid being his authentic self, and a deep inner loneliness and outward pretence take root.

If the mother had been able to share her feelings, her symptoms would have been greatly eased by knowing that thousands of other mothers suffer in this way. She would not have felt so alone. If the father had been able to share his feeling of inadequacy, he would have found freedom in the knowledge that thousands of other fathers suffer similar fears. Similarly, the student would have found the courage to stand his ground, knowing that he was not as different as he had felt, and that others in the group were not as sure of themselves as he thought.

This kind of sharing can be done on many levels. Often all we need is someone with whom we can think aloud, and who is there while we work out our own solutions. A friend on the end of a telephone may provide the sounding board which can enable us to face and articulate fears which might otherwise take hold of us. But there is also an army of people who provide a vast, essential and largely unnoticed service of listening, and being there – hairdressers, people who work in pubs, and those who work long hours in the small corner shops. Health visitors, social workers and home-helps who visit homes regularly, often provide the vital listening post that we need.

There are other ways of sharing more openly. Near my home there are two small shops where people go to buy a range of basic products. Behind the counter are dedicated human beings who not only run a business, but also provide a place where customers can gather and talk. In one, benches are put out at lunch time so that the pupils from the local comprehensive school have somewhere to sit and eat their snacks when it is cold or wet. They feel accepted. A number of pupils have built on that feeling of acceptance, and entrust their problems and fears to the proprietress, who is there day after day providing continuity and a familiar face. One day one of the teaching staff came in, insisting that she throw the pupils out during the lunch break. She told the teacher that it was her shop, that they were her customers, and that they gave her no cause for concern. By this action she preserved the trusting relationship with the young people, while maintaining her own authority. She and her family and staff continue to provide friendship and security for hundreds of teenagers.

In the other shop, a hardware store, two elderly brothers provide a similar place. They will also visit the homes of pensioners who need to have a light-bulb fitted, for example. Nothing is too small or menial. They have been burgled many times, yet their commitment causes them to stay in the district, reopen and continue their service. They are often to be found listening to someone with a problem. The atmosphere is respectful, so waiting turns into a quiet sharing. No one is to be seen drumming their fingers on the counter waiting to be served. If they are in a hurry they leave, knowing that important business is being done. It is the business of befriending.

This kind of befriending is practised by busy people. We need to examine our own kind of busy-ness, and make sure we are not using our activity to escape from closeness with others. The befriending business is a service which helps both individuals and whole communities.

Some fears are about such intimate or threatening matters that we dare not risk sharing them with anyone. A young man felt deeply betrayed when he discovered that his wife had had an affair with another man. He became frightened, then angry. He began to blame her, and then to blame himself, but he suppressed his anger and pretended to everyone that he was happily married. In private, he and his wife were unable to communicate without hurting each other more. It was not until a perceptive friend looked him in the eyes one day and said, 'You're an angry man,' that he realised what he was doing. His reluctance to share his pain at an early stage had built up to an inability to do so. His fear was paralysing him. When his friend made this observation, he felt found out and spluttered, 'I don't know what you're talking about.' But he soon capitulated, and began to feel deeply relieved. The friend accepted him, listened, and did not judge him. The anger that had been burning him up began to die down as he acknowledged it, to himself and to his friend. Now he did not feel so alone and frightened. He began to come alive again and to face his deep fears of abandonment. He discovered, in talking with his wife, that she thought he did not need or value her. She had felt rejected by his behaviour and, in her loneliness, had responded to the attentions of another man. With this new understanding, they began to draw closer, helping to heal each other. It takes courage to share fear with another in this way, but it brings wholeness – especially if it is not left too long.

There are many who have natural skills in listening to and accepting other people, yet for those of us who have not received special training, there are pitfalls we must be careful to avoid. It is important how we show our friendship to those who entrust their fears to us. In some churches, for instance, there are 'caring' people who do not help. They are the ones who, after receiving a confidence, telephone several people to share the information, 'just for prayer'. Although meant well, this is the slippery slope to gossip, and to breaking the confidentiality of the person in need. Some gossip can be harmless, but we need to exercise good judgement, and distinguish between the information that destroys another's character and that which does not.

Gossip can be a subtle form of manipulation which can surround and isolate a person in a different way. Gossips cannot be trusted, and they too are lonely people. We should take care that we don't fall into the trap of using sensitive information about other people to make friends for ourselves, especially when we feel lonely. Those relationships will be based on false ground.

There is another unhelpful response we can make and that

51

is to panic. Sometimes a person will share very deep fears, which alarm us. The unhelpful response is to jump to conclusions and, over-anxious to protect, we rush to advise. The helpful response is to be still, and to accept, enabling the person to go on at their own pace. Any further efforts at that point will divest the sufferer of what dignity they have left, of their ability to make their own choices, and to be a growing person. It can be difficult to discern a cry for help from a need to unburden, but the most important thing is to be there as a friend or colleague, and not to arrogantly assume the role of mother, father, or some kind of saviour.

Once a person came to me with a cry for help, and I needed to think carefully about my role. This gifted young woman was extremely disturbed. She said what she could, and I listened. She had been having professional help, but she had let her appointments lapse. Her husband had sent her away to the particular conference where we met, in desperation. There was nothing more he felt he could do. I encouraged her to contact her doctor again and resume the appointments. She agreed to this. I kept in touch with her, and well over a year later, after several suicide attempts, she was discharged from the hospital where she had been admitted. She has now quite recovered, and is living a very full life with a job and growing family, with no recurrence of her former terrors. She had, in the hands of professionals, been allowed to be herself, to make her own choices about what she wanted to do with her life. My role was to be someone who was there while she worked that out, and not to yield to the temptation to stop her 'doing anything silly'. I could not, if I tried. Rather than patronising protection, she needed consistent friendship from me.

Every human being needs someone alongside. We have been designed that way from the beginning. So we need to acknowledge that and then go on to find ways to help each other to be closer and more interdependent. We cannot exist without each other. We are each other's hidden benefits. We shall find our lives enriched when we can acknowledge our humanity – fears and all – to ourselves, and then know that we can share our fears with another person, whether at home, with a friend, or with a trained counsellor. Having begun to face our fears like this we shall go on to discover the excitement of taking courage, taking charge of our lives, and taking the risk of growing to maturity.

6

Facing Fear and Finding Courage

Fear is not only a feeling. It is a fact. It is part of the truth about our humanity, and proves that we are alive. If we are to face the truth, then we need to stand four-square to our fears and look straight at them, preferably with someone else. This takes courage. Half-facing our fears leaves us with only an incomplete impression of the truth, and we frighten and confuse ourselves more than we need. Fully facing them brings courage, confidence and freedom.

Many of us as children had moments when we were afraid of the dark. Even the half-light of the street lamp or the moon outside our windows would make alarming shapes which set our imaginations running, and we would pull the bedclothes closer. We would lie there with our hearts pumping from fear of what might be there, not knowing for certain who or what was outside. As a child, just after the Second World War, I had to go to bed up some dark stairs and along a passage lit by a dim light bulb. I often imagined a man with a gun lurking round the corner. If there had been a stronger light, less would have been left to my imagination. Of course there was no such person, but my fear was real enough.

Half looking at what we fear, leads us to confusion. We leave ourselves with just an impression and go on to imagine consequences, building defences in our imagination.

Facing fear is like putting on the main light. As children we found it comforting when someone came to switch on the light for us. As growing people we learn how to turn the light on for ourselves, and also for each other. However, when we continue to feel afraid, it helps to pause and acknowledge what is happening, and look properly at the suspected cause

54

of fear. This way we begin to face the truth and find courage in the process. We feel more secure, and less fearful.

Fear of the dark and of the half-light is a basic fear. So is the fear of letting go in sleep. We all go to sleep, and it is something most of us welcome. Sleep is not difficult to talk about; it is a natural activity bringing refreshment, and is necessary to life. Even sleeplessness is not a taboo subject.

Yet some people find it difficult to sleep. They toss and turn, their minds full of problems. Sleep eludes them, and they begin to worry. This anxiety turns to fear, and the cycle continues.

There are practical ways in which we can help ourselves if we do find it difficult to sleep. Some people need to unwind from the day's activities by reading, watching television or listening to the radio while they wait for sleep to take over. Sleeping pills can help to break the pattern of sleeplessness, though they should never become a habit.

If we still can't sleep, it is important to decide early what to do. To get up, to make a cup of tea, or to switch on the fire and read a book or magazine for half an hour, can often break the cycle of sleeplessness, and prevent increasing anxiety. It is comforting if there is someone else awake to talk to for a few minutes – lying awake at night can be lonely.

The fears that keep us awake, the fears of sleeplessness, are closely linked with our fear of losing control of ourselves. We have to trust and want to let go in sleep, believing that we shall wake up in the morning.

Underlying fear of the dark and of letting go in sleep is the most basic fear, that of losing control in death. We fear the process of dying ourselves, and we fear losing someone close to us in death. These fears are real and common, yet we find them hard to talk about. But talking about these fears can be like starting to breathe again. Discussing death and dying honestly is a way of confronting the mystery of it. It will help us to look at the different aspects of the fear of death and dying that frighten us.

Part of the mystery that we have to handle from childhood is what happens to the body when someone dies. Looking at the dead body of a person has become difficult because we are not used to it, and the days of leaving the corpse in a coffin in the front room have largely passed in this country. The nearest experience we have is at a funeral or the lying-in-state of a distinguished person; even then, the lid is firmly nailed down and we are left only with our imagination and with memories. Death is shrouded in mystery and hushed tones. We grant ourselves a half-look at the meaning of death, and so gain just an impression of what it means. Consequently many of us are frightened of talking about it.

Recently, in Liverpool we faced sudden and large-scale tragedy when ninety-five football fans were crushed to death on the terraces at Hillsborough. The shock and sense of bereavement was widespread, and everyone needed to talk about it. Even the Director of Social Services, David Mason, made it public that he needed to seek the help of a counsellor himself. The Liverpool Football Club, directors, players and their wives, opened their premises, and spent time with bereaved families, and it felt natural for us all to share our stories and grief with one another. There was no embarrassment, no hushed whispers, but a quiet understanding atmosphere that meant we encouraged one another while the full impact of the news took effect.

So it is important to face the fact of death; then we shall find courage. Death is indeed a real threat to life, and therefore an enemy. It is something to resist until it actually claims us in old age, extreme sickness, accident or war. It is to be resisted because life is a gift and to be treasured. If we gave up this treasure, surrendering our will to live, then the human race, the human spirit, would no longer exist. We would soon be back to the darkness and chaos of time before the world began. Death is not only an enemy; it is always a tragedy when someone dies.

Christ recognised tragedy when his friend Lazarus died. He expressed indignation and grief openly when he heard the news. When later it was his turn to die, he faced the full force of separation from those closest to him: from his Father, his mother and his close friends, his family and colleagues.

For those gathered at the foot of his cross, there was a grim reality to face. They were grieving and bereaved people. As

56

well as losing their Lord, they had lost a son and a close friend at the peak of his life. They had to feel the loss in order to let him go. To pretend that he was still alive at that moment would have transported them into realms of fantasy. To have begun to discuss the resurrection just then would have been denying Christ his true humanity, and also denying their own. They needed to face the facts so as to become fully alive, allowing the human responses to come through. Any other response would have meant pretence and prevented them from having any opportunity to show love and comfort to each other. Christ noticed the need for this while he was dying, and commended his mother and his friend to each other. As well as experiencing his own pain, he knew how hurt they felt, and acknowledged their humanity.

For the Christian, the tragedy is not the end of the story. We believe in new life after death. We believe in resurrection. But it is unhealthy to skip too quickly over the feelings of loss and tragedy that bereaved people experience. We shall feel a sense of loss, and an aching void, if we have been close to the person who has died. So we need to acknowledge those feelings in ourselves and also in other people. It is part of acknowledging the whole truth about a person.

That is why funerals are so important. They are times when we give each other the opportunity to grieve and also to express our faith in God and the future together. Death can then be transformed, very gently, from tragedy to triumph, as and when we are ready.

A funeral is an occasion when the community comes together to remember the dead person, and to support the bereaved family. It provides a natural opportunity to talk unhurriedly together and to share experiences in an open context. Ideally, the clergy offer an understanding and listening presence. Death can be looked at openly for an hour or so. This helps to bring courage to those who mourn, enabling them not to feel alone, as they attempt to face their loss.

As well as facing death at funerals, it helps to talk with others. Until recently I was ashamed of admitting that I was afraid of seeing a dead body. I was encouraged when I talked about this with an elderly person who shared the fear, and, in her late seventies, told me that she had not seen one either. We can prepare ourselves much better if we can talk about death, bringing the same energy to this subject as we do when talking about birth. Birth and death are inevitable; they are facts of life and they both need to be faced more openly.

A married couple I knew faced a crisis, and found they were avoiding the real issue. The man was terminally ill with cancer. He knew the truth about his condition, but was afraid of what would happen to his wife when he was gone. She knew that he had not long to live, yet was afraid of telling him, not realising he already knew. She shared her fears with a visitor, who encouraged them to talk openly with each other about how they were feeling. Finally they shared their fears with each other. Then they were able to spend the last few weeks of the man's life in open communication and love, making plans together for her and for their children, finding the courage which flowed from facing the truth together.

A positive and open approach to death, as to life, is the way of the l'Arche Community. L'Arche, founded by Jean Vanier, has a number of houses throughout Europe. In each house lives a small community comprising an equal number of severely mentally handicapped people and assistants. One of the keystones of l'Arche's philosophy is the need of preserve the dignity of every human being, whoever they are. From their broken lives, the severely handicapped people bring wholeness and acceptance to those who might regard themselves as 'normal'.

One day, in one of the Liverpool houses, a man called George died. George was severely handicapped, and his friends in the house wanted to know what his death and dying was all about. Just before he died, George was visited by every member of the household, and talked freely about his feelings and fears. When he died, everyone was allowed to see his body and to go together to his funeral. One of the community wanted to write him a note. He was allowed to take it in and put it in George's dead hand. Facing death as naturally as this helped everyone to share openly in what could have been a bewildering tragedy. This openness also brought a closeness to George which helped him to die with dignity, knowing he was not alone. They encouraged one another, while facing the truth together.

If we don't talk about our fear of death we deprive not only ourselves but also our children of a healthy facing of reality. They will grow up unprepared for loss, and more likely to build their understanding on snippets of second-hand truth filtered down from people further away from their immediate experience. If a member of the family or community dies, it is more helpful when there is no pretence or camouflage. Each of us needs the opportunity to relate to a particular death in whichever way we find comfortable, and to talk about it openly.

Facing death is about facing loss; we fear losing control. Losing control over our lives or bodies or possessions is not death, but is the cause of a fundamental and healthy fear, and one which needs facing. Each day we face situations which feel like little deaths, and which demand courage and determination.

The response of children to loss, as to death, is direct. I lost a favourite and treasured baby doll as a toddler. No matter where we looked, Ingrid was nowhere to be found. How I missed her! Days later, out for a walk with my mother and younger brother, I spotted something lying under a high, clipped hedge. It was Ingrid. But my joy in finding her was marred because not only was she soaking wet, but her round pink face was covered in a thousand cracks. The shock of seeing her like this is still with me. She disintegrated, and the feeling of loss was compounded. As a result, I became more possessive of my things, determined not to lose anything again.

Losing precious things, as children or as adults, hurts, and we become afraid of more loss. But losing people is even more painful. A child may temporarily lose a parent while out shopping, or later be parted from loved ones at home when admitted to hospital. Deep feelings of being deserted and abandoned may develop. A great deal of my childhood was very happy, but experiences like these, together with losing my father to serve in the war, and later learning to 'lose' him to the ministry of the Church set up real fears of being left with no parents at all.

When I went to boarding school, I remember well the dragging feeling in the pit of my stomach as we drew nearer to the school. There was no alternative; I had to find courage to face leaving home. I began to grow up, but I also learned how to hide my feelings instead of sharing them openly; not even my parents knew till much later.

Part of what we fear is that one loss will lead to another, and that little deaths will lead on to larger ones.

This process of loss can lead us to be defensive in adult life. The 'little deaths' continue for adults. Rejection after a job interview, losing a job altogether, losing a partner or parent through divorce, are only a few examples. Feelings of loss can make us afraid of more loss, and so we take steps to protect ourselves. Even so, at unguarded moments we find the old dread of being abandoned rising, and this can lead to angry, defensive behaviour.

It can feel like a little death for me when, for example, I have written an important letter containing an invitation or request, or made repeated telephone calls and there is no reply. I can become irritated and even angry, especially in the middle of a busy period; I blame the person at the other end for inefficiency. A harsh response like this is a sign that I feel in danger of losing control of my day's programme, and of losing the person I am trying to contact. Sometimes I feel forgotten or abandoned. I find it helpful then to acknowledge that fear of losing control. But while the responsibility to deal with the fear creatively remains mine, the feelings of loss are still real and part of me, and need to be acknowledged.

Such a loss occurred recently. During the writing of this book I trusted myself professionally to my editor. She was quietly and steadily supportive; her presence had become important to me. So it was with dismay that I picked up the telephone, to hear that she was leaving to take up a new post. She rang with the news herself. I felt stranded and hurt; her decision was difficult to accept. The trusting relationship was in jeopardy, and in a matter of moments my fears surfaced. I feared that my work would not be completed and that I would not be able to cope with this failure. My editor's leaving felt like a death.

But then I decided to look at the facts, while allowing myself to recognise my feelings. My editor had not made this decision to hurt me, but needed to live her own life. She had already directed me to the new editor, and she had rung me personally instead of writing. I was not stranded – and I could share my worry. My husband was in, so I told him and he hugged me and said he knew I would ride it. I rang a close friend; she encouraged me to live through the feelings of hurt and desertion and not to apologise for them, as they were part of me.

Being able to admit I was angry and upset, was part of facing the truth, accepting my humanity; and talking about the problem freed me to look at the facts and accept them.

Very quickly the new editor phoned me to make a date to meet, and I was back on firm ground. I was no longer angry or hurt; I rang the departing editor to thank her and to wish her well in her new job.

Within the hour, I was back at the desk, scribbling away and determined to finish. Through accepting myself and taking responsibility for my fearful feelings, I was a little wiser, and more confident.

Loss can hurt, so we build defences, to cushion ourselves against a sudden assault on our senses, our bodies or on the lives of those close to us. We fear losing little bits of our life, and try to defend ourselves against being hurt. Instead of putting our energies into living, we concentrate on surviving, and develop a siege mentality, expecting trouble. 'How are you?' we are asked. 'Surviving,' is the reply.

We are not here to survive, but to live; it is fear that reduces us to this level of survival. We fear being overwhelmed by work, by family circumstances or by deeper things inside ourselves that we are unable to conquer. Our space feels crowded; so we put up barriers. In public we joke desperately, and in private we sink down despairingly.

But there is another way of living. Each small threat can

either become a reason to withdraw in negative defensiveness, or it can become a new opportunity to discover how life can follow death over and over again.

Making mistakes can feel like small threats, but is part of being human. Learning to walk, we expect to stumble. But once we can walk we do not expect to stumble any more. We have come to believe that all there is to life is walking on the straight, flat pavement of our childhood. But there are bumpy pavements, and hills and mountains to scale, and we deceive ourselves if we believe the way forward holds no difficulties. We shall trip and sometimes fall; it is important to recognise this and also to remember that we are not alone.

Being afraid of tripping and falling is another problem. We imagine that one day we shall not survive on the journey. We imagine that one day we shall trip and find we cannot get up, and will be alone and without help.

One of the more serious 'little deaths' we can face is the process of ageing. Like death, this is natural; like death we can meet it with acceptance or with fear. Many elderly people have much to teach us. Those who are not afraid of dying, or of talking about it, have come to terms with reality. If we know elderly people like that, then we are fortunate. But there are many others who sink into a confused and half-dead state of mind, believing themselves to be left alone and unwanted. Often they feel totally out of touch with younger people. But elderly and younger people don't need to approach each other in a state of fear; they could help each other to find courage and a healthy approach to old age and dying. The difference to be observed in retirement homes where the elderly people have been given a place of dignity, and people to talk to, is marked. There, they are more alert and interested in the world around them.

We need to keep in regular touch with elderly people; they need our support when their strength is failing. Most of all, they need someone there when facing the end of their lives.

Sometimes there are fears about our health that we may shrink from facing.

Fear of cancer stalks many hearts. Those who are ill with cancer fear they have a kind that cannot be cured; they are afraid of dying of cancer. The imagined consequence, that we will die, becomes so unbearable that we turn away from the truth and pretend that there is nothing to worry about. We try to be brave and cheerful. Facing the truth with courage means sharing the facts early with a partner, doctor or trusted friend. The truth might hold some welcome surprises. It will always bring freedom.

With my own previous history of cancer, I became anxious when I discovered a small lump on my scalp. Fear crept in, and I kept the information to myself. Sometime later, I noticed that it was bigger, and realised that I could no longer ignore it. I shared the facts with my husband and one or two friends, and made an appointment to see the doctor. Later, and with considerable relief, I walked out of the hospital without the lump, and only a few stitches. It had been a benign cyst and harmless. Facing the fear privately, and then with friends gave me the courage to do something about it.

Another major fear is of mental breakdown; many people are afraid of losing their minds. They often appear to be among the most sensible, integrated and gifted human beings. But something has caused them to become afraid and ashamed; they have isolated themselves, while anxiously watching others; they feel alone and different. While people like this struggle inwardly with lack of confidence, outwardly they often compensate by appearing supremely in control. This cannot go on for ever, and there comes a time when real breakdown occurs.

When we feel like that, it takes courage to share our fears with others. But we need to tell someone whom we trust. If they listen well, and accept us fully, then they will not reach for the nearest telephone to commit us to mental hospital. This listening will begin to allay our real fear of going mad, and will bring a sense of proportion back into our lives.

A professional man told me that he was alarmed when he woke one night, trembling with fear. It destroyed his sleep, and he began to wonder whether there was something wrong with his mind. He confided in his wife who listened and accepted his fears. Some nights later, the trembling returned, and he got up to make a cup of tea. He then bravely faced his fear of going to a mental hospital and said to himself with a touch of humour, 'Oh well, if I have to go to hospital, that is where I must go!' Immediately, the trembling stopped. By taking courage soon enough, and facing his fear with another person, he freed himself.

A fear of marriage breakdown is also common. If our marriage is under strain, it is easy to imagine that the partnership is finished for ever. Fear of complete breakdown drives us to keep quiet, hoping that things will work themselves out. We become too fearful to talk to our partner or to a close friend. So we close the door to possible support or guidance. Yet, underneath, we feel fragmented and weary with pretending as we battle privately with the fear. This way we damage ourselves, and one another.

There is another way. It involves taking courage early enough, and discussing our fears openly, facing the facts before they develop into dangerous fantasies.

One of the most alarming fears in a breaking marriage is the possibility that one partner will leave the home. This common fear of being forsaken tells us an important truth. We were never designed to be alone, even as adults. We need each other if we are to live and create; without each other, we perish in fragmented isolation.

In all these situations one of the best ways of getting things into proportion is by using our sense of humour. Laughing, joking and clowning play a vital part in our development.

Just as people who smile are not necessarily happy, so those who joke are not always finding life funny. But a sense of humour is a useful tool in our human equipment. It is the ability to stand away from something serious and see the funny side. A sense of humour transcends and lifts us above ourselves. For some people life is such a crushing load, that they need plenty of joking to absorb or fend off the pain. It is a necessary aid to life. But we need to recognise whether a joker is trying to tell us something serious which is hidden in the jest. Cartoons, for instance, are serious communications, and can hold deep meaning. But it does not stop us from laughing affectionately at some of the people portrayed. Those people should include ourselves, naturally.

Children have a natural sense of humour, and we need to rediscover our own. Whenever people have felt particularly afraid, as in war-time, or in hospital, laughing has helped to bring a sense of proportion. Laughter loosens the tension and enables us to take courage to face our fears.

All fears are real, but the objects of our fears can either be real or imagined. When they are imagined, we cross bridges in our minds before we come to them, preparing ourselves for possible setbacks or attacks. John Bunyan illustrated this in *Pilgrim's Progress*. In his dream Bunyan saw that Christian was confronted at one stage of his journey to the Celestial City by two huge snarling lions. They were barring his way forward. He was frightened, and did not know how he could continue his journey without losing his life in the process. He was tempted to turn back but, as he looked, he saw the porter at the gate, Watchful. Watchful encouraged him to continue, telling him that the lions were chained up and would not harm him if he kept to a straight path between them. So he kept bravely on, trembling as he heard the lions roaring. He could see that he would not be touched or harmed if he did not waver. Courage triumphed over fear, and he went through unharmed.

Courage is waiting for us to take hold of it. It is nearer when we are in touch with ourselves, when we know what we want; it eludes us when we are in two minds. Making decisions is courageous; we find that the paralysis of controlling fear gives way, freeing us to enjoy the adventure ahead. We too can know the fulfilling and creative result of confronting our fears, sharing them and deciding what we really want.

The air was soft and warm, the sky a brilliant blue and the water, clear and inviting. My husband was putting finishing touches to his painting and our two friends were claiming the last moments of a perfect holiday to stretch out in the sun. I was standing on the edge of the pool, determined to jump, by myself, into the water to fulfil a life-time's ambition. I had waited for fifty-two years to do this, and somehow, up until now, I hadn't found the courage. There was always something in the way. I would find an excuse and put it off to another day. Today, there was no excuse.

Voices from the past wafted in: 'Go on, Mum, it's easy. Look at me.' Or, 'Just jump', and 'There's nothing to be afraid of.' Pictures of children flinging themselves into the water, squealing with delight, bobbing up like corks, wet and triumphant, taunted me. Other, less positive, voices lurked in the lovely air: 'You're a coward.' 'You should have managed a simple thing like that at your age. Just look at the children.' 'It's not important. Give up, and do something you really want to do. Don't make an exhibition of yourself. Give up.' My whole body began to tremble.

I was both terrified and excited. Supposing I forgot to hold my nose? Supposing I slipped? Supposing I swallowed gallons of water and couldn't breathe? Supposing I had an accident and died? That was it. The risk was too great.

But I wanted to live. And living isn't about giving up, it is about making things happen. It is about facing fear and finding courage. It is about discovery. No one was going to jump in for me. I had to do it alone. Just then my two friends came up to join me. They wanted to know what I had in mind, so I told them. They beamed with delight. They shared my excitement. I felt they also shared my terror. Neither of them made moves to push me in, or trick me. Neither of them jumped in to show me. Neither of them laughed at me. I felt they wanted to share in some way. I continued to dither, still determined not to walk away. Suddenly one of them said, 'Supposing we jumped in together?' It was then that I made up my mind. There were no excuses left. I would jump, break a leg, take a risk, drown if necessary. After a count of three, my feet left the edge of the pool, my arms flying, hit the

66

water, touched the bottom, and up to the sunlight. A few feet away, my friend had surfaced too. She didn't know what that small gesture meant to me. Her loving companionship, enthusiasm and zest for life gave me life, and I fulfilled my ambition. I swam to the edge of the pool, leapt out and jumped in again, alone this time. The fear evaporated; I felt fully alive.

To Risk is to Create

When I became a bishop's wife, one of the challenges to face was meeting large groups of people several times a week. I would accompany my husband to services and other public events. But while I was used to meeting a large crowd at our church in east London, they were the same people every week, and we had taken the opportunity to become well acquainted over many years. Now, the crowd and the context were different every week, yet I remained the same. Afraid of putting my foot in it, during the refreshments afterwards, I would quietly attend, hoping that I wouldn't be in the way. Not wanting to be 'pushy', I did not introduce myself to anyone and waited for someone else to move first.

Eventually I decided to do something about the situation. I knew what I did want, and that was to share in an open conversation and be accepted for myself. The only way through this dilemma was to change my behaviour. Instead of acting like a shrinking violet, out of fear, I would have to risk my reputation for being a quiet, decorous person, and put more effort into being myself, which I believed to be lively, responsive and not always quiet.

So, inch by inch, I became myself. At each event, gathering my courage, I would boldly approach a group and say, 'Hello, I'm Grace Sheppard. Who are you?' My heart would beat wildly; I was battling with the self-judgement that I had developed as a young Christian years ago which had tried to rub out the 'I', and then passively let Christ shine through. It was painful, and involved effort, but deep down I knew I was being true to myself, and the people I met responded in rewarding ways. Gradually I came to believe that my personality was not something to be ashamed of after all. People talked more freely once they had got over the embarrassment of talking to a bishop's wife. I felt freer too, and now it is second nature. I no longer fear the changing crowds of faces and I enjoy the company of each person I meet, particularly if they feel free to be themselves too.

Once we have found the courage to confront our fears, and share them with another person, we begin to feel more alive. The paralysis that gripped us, gradually lets go and life returns. We begin to face the future with new energy.

Facing the future becomes exciting when we remember that we are made in God's image. We are born to create something new and unique. At the moment of our birth we confront a new world where we need equipment we didn't need before. Our lungs fill with air, our eyes open, and our instincts begin to function. We break into a new atmosphere. As well as feeling the comfort of our mother's breast, we also begin to know the pain of colic. It makes us cry because it hurts. Our instinct to live drives us on and, with pain as a new factor, we discover new responses. One of these responses is fear.

So, as new babies we become fully alive. But it is risky to be born, and a matter of life and death. We cannot survive for long alone. Our basic needs have to be met by someone. As we develop, it becomes increasingly difficult to grow, to play, and to create if our basic needs are not met. So to be fully alive and creative we begin to take risks, gradually learning to exercise our own wills, and providing for our own needs. We exchange dependence on our mother for interdependency, where we relate to each other in the wider world. From the womb to the outside world, we take our lives in our hands, learning how to leave home and to take care of ourselves. We go on to learn how to channel our energy into creating something new and ordered. At the same time we recognise our potential for causing pain to other people, and even for creating chaos.

As well as realising these two alternatives, there is a third choice, which is to do nothing. But doing nothing, like the other two, produces consequences. What matters, is identifying which decision we wish to make. Our resolve to take a

calculated risk or to make a decision is weakened by unacknowledged fear. Fear of pain, or of not surviving, takes
control. We become uncertain of who we are and what we
want to do. Prolonged uncertainty is dangerous, as we run
the risk of allowing ourselves to become overwhelmed with
fear.

It will help through uncertain times to remember what we
set out to do in the first place. It will help to remember our
commitment to the task we have chosen. It will help also to
know that we are free to change our minds and to make a
new decision along the way, without feeling we have failed.
There is nothing necessarily harmful or wrong in reversing
a decision. Sometimes it will be essential that we do, as
circumstances change. Setting out to sea in a boat to fish may
be what we have decided to do. It would be foolish to ignore
all new weather reports of gale force winds and storm conditions, if we realise we are not equipped to face them. It
would be common sense to decide to turn back. What can be
harmful is to allow ourselves to waver for too long, allowing
fear to creep in and take charge. In the boat, we would have
risked being sunk, if we had not taken note and made a sound
decision.

Taking risks does not come naturally to everyone. The
more fearful we are, the less likely we are to try something
new. We settle for the comfort of the familiar, shielding ourselves from the insecurity of the unknown. Opting for comfort
means that our creative energies are channelled into stream-
lining our securities. Frightened people often create warm,
welcoming homes. Like an oyster, we stay alive, and growing,
but at the same time we build layers of shell to protect the
vulnerable treasure inside. We grow into ourselves, shut away
from other people.

But we are not oysters. We are people with wills of our
own. Choosing to peer out from our barricades of safety is
our privilege. When we feel more secure, we take a peep to
see if we dare try something new. It is like a small boy I
knew, who hid behind the armchair when 'Doctor Who' was
being shown on television. He was both excited and terrified
at once. He would peep to see whether he could survive

another shock to his system, exhilarated enough to stay in the room, frightened enough to keep the armchair between him and the television set. We are like that. We hover between wanting and not wanting, not daring to open both eyes. Instead of saying, 'I won't', we begin to say 'I can't'.

The Victorian saying, 'There's no such word as can't', rings in our ears. Its harsh and dismissive note can, if we let it, make us tremble all the more. There is such a word, and there is such a feeling. As Christians, some of us grew up believing that the verse, 'I can do all things through Christ who strengthens me,' meant that, if we wanted to, we could achieve anything with Christ's help. Of course there is truth in that. But we are not called as individuals to do everything, or to rule the world. Unreal expectations of ourselves as individuals put impossible weights on us. No wonder we sometimes feel we 'can't'. As Christians, and as a church, we are not called to be God himself by ourselves, but together instead to reflect his nature.

We need to set each other free from our feelings of being trapped, by acceptance of one another as we are. We need to encourage each other in the risky business of being alive by being there. Most important, we need to find ways of encouraging ourselves.

When we feel fearful, it helps to remember that the facts are kind. For a Christian the facts include the truth that God is near, and that his imprint is on all his creation. He is a God who loves us without making conditions, and who designed us to be fully alive, and to exercise our wills. He is not a dominant ruler, but wants to live alongside us as a friend who does not desert us when the going gets tough. Christ's coming demonstrated the facts about God, his Father.

Recently, I became frightened of making the trip to London by train. I lost my self-confidence and felt paralysed when approaching the barrier. I was poised for flight. Was my old trouble returning? Would I have to surmount the problem all over again? I knew I couldn't walk the length of the platform. But I remembered that I had friends and family who loved and understood me. I was physically healthy. No one would

71

punish me for not making the journey. But I still could not board the train.

The night before my second attempt at the journey, my husband and I entertained a visitor. Uncharacteristically, I found myself telling him about my terror of the next day. He listened with marked acceptance. Talking to him like that helped my husband and me with the problem. We felt supported, and I decided to try again. I remembered that the passengers on the train were like me, human, and with their own challenges and fears to face; we were all made in God's image.

The next day dawned, and I gathered my papers as usual and prepared to go to the station. Walking from the car to the barrier was difficult. I felt there were heavy weights on my ankles, and I thought I would fall. It was the same on the platform. As the train pulled in to the station I opened the carriage door. I remembered that if I looked, I would find aspects of God in the people on the train. This spurred me on. I wanted to be with them, and realised they were more likely to be friends, than enemies. I stepped on to the train, and immediately my fear was transformed into something more positive. I felt whole again, and alive.

The journey flew by, and the people at our table struck up a lively conversation. At our destination, I walked the length of the platform feeling inches taller. By remembering the kind facts, and by trusting myself to the goodness of God, as it was to be found in the people and things in the world outside, wholeness and new life had come to me, and I had grown a little more.

For a woman, the time after the children have grown up and left home is often like launching out on a journey. When the children leave home, some mothers find that their reason for living departs with them, though this is true only if she had previously given all her time and energy to them. The quiet and order she had craved when her children were there become oppressive in their absence. She is left wondering how best to spend her time, and this can be confusing.

Such a woman will be faced with a choice. She can channel her energies into caring for and protecting her husband, sometimes treating him as if he were another child. Or she can think about involving herself in some other activity, exercising old skills or acquiring new ones.

There are many women who find great fulfilment in keeping an open home, long after the children have left. These homes are a haven to many people; they provide a welcome for all-comers, and are like bright lights in a forsaken wilderness. Communities need places like this, but unless there is careful negotiation between husband and wife, they can become exhausted strangers to one another. If they allow the press of the crowd to dominate their lives, they may become like hollow shells when the last visitor has left. They run the risk of long-term estrangement privately, while offering friendship and welcome to others.

Some women take up a completely new profession, while others enjoy the opportunities that are offered through the second-chance learning courses in colleges and universities. Many take up voluntary work, as I did when I joined the Liverpool Family Service Unit, or join an organisation like the Mothers Union, which is a huge, caring and efficient, world-wide organisation with branches in varied countries.

Whether married or not, and whether a man or a woman, we need to look out for factors that weaken our resolve to break into something new. Our resolve is weakened by listening too long to cautious voices. We shall never learn from our mistakes if we do not make any. Caution is necessary to life, but staying too long with the amber light will lead us to stop altogether. Thinking about making a journey is a good beginning, but after a while comes the time to make a decision – either to go or not to go. Just to stay at home, undecided, opens up the way for fear to creep in and to take control. Our good intentions need to be transformed into action, otherwise we become static and unproductive. The risk of committing ourselves to anything or anyone is great, whether it is to try painting a picture for the first time, or to share our lives with another person. The fear of failure is present but, without decisive action, the opportunity to create something new and fulfilling is thwarted. Good ideas and good intentions are only a beginning. Starting something new takes courage and, like having a baby, involves action and hard work.

When I was approached to write a book, I felt it would be too risky. The cautious thoughts crowded in. I might not be able to finish what I had started. What would I write about? Would I be able to express myself? Would I have the discipline required? 'No', I thought, 'I can't'. But as well as the fears, I detected small stirrings of excitement. In discussing it with my husband and close friends, I was encouraged to think about the idea further. So I began to warm to the idea, feeling a mixture of excitement and terror. Like the small boy behind the armchair, I glanced fitfully at the proposition. It became increasingly attractive, and I grew in confidence. I agreed to meet the editor, and the ideas began to flow. But ideas are only the beginning, and are useless unless put into practice. The book would not write itself.

Creation involves action and effort, and I decided to try, risking myself in the process. Writing a book for the first time is like jumping in the deep end of a pool, making a journey or painting a picture. We set out on an adventure, not knowing where it will lead. It becomes part of a life of faith.

Good ideas and good intentions followed up by decisive action create results, though there will be some pain in the process. We shall have to put in some effort, to experience the rewards of risking. But first we need to discover what we want to do.

For some Christians, wanting anything is regarded as selfish and greedy, and therefore wrong. Discovering what we want can take some time; we are unsure whether it is all right to want anything at all for ourselves. So we punish ourselves, feeling we have sinned. We want to do God's will but remain unsure about our own desires, so we refuse to give ourselves the dignity of those who can make their own decisions. In striving to be perfect we turn away from the responsibility that would be ours if we made a firm decision; we are unsure that what we want is good enough for God. We are uncertain that we are good enough for any person or task. So we become indecisive, passive individuals, waiting for guidance from outside and unwilling to take risks. We fear disapproval for not being perfect, so fancy that God can work on in spite of us. Without realising it, we deny the very humanity we have been given at our birth, stifling our feelings and responses. It is less painful that way, or so it appears.

Often, pursuing the less painful way means that we relieve ourselves from facing our imperfections. This way we also prevent others from seeing that we are human too. This is no service to them, or to Christ, and we harm ourselves in the process. Christ wants us to be fully human, rich in our differences. He wants us to exercise our wills as well as our bodies and spirits, in full, active partnership with him and with each other. If we made no mistakes, we would learn nothing about the value of his presence when we fall – his unconditional love would hold no meaning for us. Risking means that we will make the wrong decision sometimes, or even disturb another person, but at least we shall be taking responsibility for ourselves and becoming wiser in the process.

Playing safe is not wrong, but means that when we cease to want to take risks, we have settled for a life without disturbance. Like a pond with a calm surface, neither disturbed nor disturbing, we become stagnant. We need to be clear whether that is the kind of life we really want. We have only one life; others are managing theirs around us. Something inside us longs to join in, and then we shrink back into our shells, afraid to take part. We prefer to do our own thing, feeling safer. So we stay at home, down in our bunkers, shy, lonely and depressed.

Taking part in outside life can be daunting. Like children in the playground, we want to join in the fun, but are afraid we will not be strong enough to stand up to the bullies. We would like to be like other people, but are afraid that we will not fit in, that we will be different, standing out like sore thumbs. We fear ridicule. We begin to imagine the world is full of strong and successful people. We lose heart, feeling we cannot be like that. So we decide to keep our heads down, avoiding danger.

But facing danger is where we find courage. We don't have to do it all in one go. First we must examine our position, starting from where we are, and honestly answering the question, 'Who am I?' In asking this, we need to distinguish it from other quite different questions, like 'Who do I think I am?' or 'Who ought I to be?'.

At the beginning of this chapter, I mentioned my venture to draw closer to groups of people on public occasions, by introducing myself early on. Before taking the courage to tell them my name like that, it was important to be quite sure I was telling the truth as simply as possible to myself.

This truth involved acknowledging my name, my history, and my relationship to my husband, who happened to be a bishop. It involved honest acknowledgement of my feelings, including fears of criticism, ridicule, and the fear of failure to meet other people's expectations. It also involved acknowledging what I wanted, which was to be closer to people, in as genuine a meeting as possible under the circumstances, getting to know each other as fellow human beings in the short time available.

Having established what I wanted, and examined where I stood, my ground was firmer, and I was ready to entrust myself to others in this way. After years of habitual waiting in public places for others to move first, I began to change my ways. This felt awkward initially, but the shyness soon wore off, and meeting people has become an enriching experience instead of the threat it used to be. Less human people have become more human, and superhuman people have become more like me. We have the choice whether to risk our lives by coming out inch by inch and together, or to stay put, safe for the time being, but trapped and alone.

This inching forward took for me time and effort. It was real work, and I was often too anxious or tired to try. But the rewards continue to be great in terms of human exchange and closeness. My expectations of myself are now more realistic, instead of feeling driven by fear to be 'the perfect bishop's wife'. Now, for instance, when my feet are cold, I will wear a pair of comfortable boots instead of battling on in a pair of smart shoes, pretending that bishops' wives are immortal, and never have cold feet.

People who suffer from extreme levels of fear do so for good reasons, and should not be told to 'snap out of it'. They may be 'resting' from their particular battle, by withdrawing from those parts of life where they feel most vulnerable. Most of all, they will need to know that they are not alone, and that it is possible to grow towards a place of wholeness in the company of other people who can stand by them, and who also have fears to face. But it will take time. We need to stop chivvying each other to grow up, and learn instead to be more patient, remembering that growth is gradual and relatively slow. Each of us has an area of life where we feel more confident, where we can afford to take more risks, finding courage along the way. This way we allow one another to grow at our own pace – it will sometimes need patience, like nurturing a valued plant.

Outside my south-facing kitchen window, just below eye-level, is a bed of winter-flowering irises. I divided each clump from the original, which came from my mother-in-law's garden. Dividing them and planting them there was a calculated risk. I was clear what I wanted, which was to create a mass of the soft purple blooms to cheer us during the winter months. The position was good, and I was advised that they would take time to bloom after being divided. Year after year went by, with only a handful of blooms, till I wondered whether to give up and move them elsewhere, but I decided to be patient a while longer. This year, as before, I peered hopefully into the bushy foliage for signs of the pointed pencil-like buds. Then gradually they came, scores of them, inch by inch, unfolding into whole beautiful, purple blooms. Patience was rewarded, and the risk of transplanting created new signs of life.

I am thankful for the patience and care of those who stood by me during the more testing times of growing when I was too frightened to leave my home. I feel like one of those iris buds.

8

The Rewards of Risking

The police had been informed, and our neighbours had been warned. The garden was looking cared for, colourful, and inviting. My small band of helpers looked at each other expectantly. It was five to two and everyone was in position, waiting for the hour to strike. I had dreamed of this moment for years, and at last our Liverpool garden was being opened to the public.

At two o'clock we opened the big white gate. But the pavement was empty, and people should have been queueing by now. I felt a mixture of elation and apprehension. We were hoping for hundreds. At half past two, my apprehension deepened. Only two people had arrived in half an hour. By the end of the afternoon over one hundred and twenty tickets had been sold, and all the teas had been eaten. Visitors had left smiling, clutching a plant to take home and praising the scones. The helpers were pleased, but deep down I was disappointed as I had hoped for more.

Three years and five events later, the numbers had not changed, so privately I decided that the next would be our last attempt. This time it was May Bank Holiday, and the day was sunny and warm. At two o'clock, there was a crowd of eager faces at the gate, and by three o'clock I knew that the tide had turned. Two hundred, five hundred, seven hundred . . . nine hundred and still arriving! The teas ran out, more ice-cream had to be bought. 'This is better than the Garden Festival,' said one. The feeling of reward for risking such a venture was real. My reward was not just the cheque we were able to send to charity, but a new confidence, replacing the apprehension. The commitment to stay with the dream was rewarded.

It is important to dream. We are built with a vital piece of equipment – called our imagination. With it we form pictures both of what we hope for or dread, and also of what we think we can or cannot do. Sometimes, what we think we want to do needs close scrutiny, if we are not to live in a fantasy world. On the other hand, what we imagine we do not want to do also needs closer inspection, as we may discover a rich store of experience there that is actually within our reach.

My picture of opening the garden was quite clear in my imagination although I had never done anything like it before. Bathed in sun, children would be rolling down the grassy banks, and playing houses under the weeping willow tree. Pensioners would be wandering, unhurriedly, pointing out some new plant in the flower beds. My picture included young parents relaxing on the lawns while their children played contentedly nearby. A band would be playing while tea was being served, and there would be fresh flowers from the garden on each table.

A dream or vision provides a sense of direction and something to hope for. By allowing our imaginations to soar, we can increase the possibilities of knowing what we want to do, and where we want to go. Young people especially need to be given room to dream, and imagination goes on working in later life. We all dream of how things might be, or could be from time to time. We live in hope.

But dreaming by itself can become sterile, and we need to link dreams with action. Sometimes we need to risk the dream by gently taking it apart to see if there is a chance that it could come true. If I had simply kept my ideas about the garden to myself, they would have gone round till I felt muddled and demotivated. I would have come to believe that I would never put my bright ideas into practice. My dream would fade. Like theory without practice, and faith without works, dreams with no action can have a deadening effect on human beings.

But in every creative experience there come moments of testing. We can allow dreaming and planning to go on too long. Inevitably, snags appear, and we allow ourselves to be wrapped up in details. Like sleeping Gulliver, we discover that we have unwittingly permitted little bonds of fear to creep in and bind us, effectively preventing us from moving forward into action.

Yet dreams provide vision and something to hope for, and are an essential ingredient for growth. Our imagination goes on working whether we like it or not, and needs an outlet from time to time. When I shared my garden dream with my friends, gradually unfolding it to see if it could be realised, we found that there would be practical implications. But my friends and I, together with George, the gardener, set to work, and the energy flowed and the enthusiasm mounted. I continued to dream of a thousand people. This gave me something to work for.

It is important to go on risking and creating something new, if we want to be alive, to grow, and to enjoy the results.

We need to take decisive action early if we are to prevent worries from binding us, bringing destructive, negative results. Frightening experiences can creep up on us unawares, but there is often something we can do to prevent them getting an uncontrollable grip on our lives, causing us to panic. We need to acknowledge quite simply how we feel, then find a trusted friend to talk to. By acting decisively, we begin the process of cutting ourselves free from the fear that binds us. This is decisive action.

Taking action though, still means we run the risk of losing control. When we start to open up our dreams or vision of what we want to do with other people, we risk rejection by those who wish to have nothing to do with our bright ideas. We risk ridicule from those who think they know better, and think we are stupid to try. We even risk insignificance if the whole plan falls to the ground and fails. After all, what we have been dreaming may not appeal to anyone else. They may laugh at our ideas, and walk away or, with blank expression, leave us feeling more lonely than when we had only our fantasy for company. We begin to allow ourselves to be frightened more than we need. But as I found with my garden enterprise, people are more generous than we think, and, more often than not, are waiting to support someone who takes the initiative.

So we need to take courage and do something about our dreams, ideas and even our nightmares. If we want a good dream to be fulfilled, we need to begin by entrusting it to another person. It is like unwrapping a parcel marked 'fragile', when we undo the knots and gingerly pull back the paper revealing the precious contents. Is the dream the same, now that it has seen the light of day? Little by little we look together at the implications of our hopes, and introduce reality to an imagined picture. We give the idea a chance to be grounded, to take root. Once this has begun to happen there emerges the opportunity to create something new and dynamic that others can share. Almost certainly it will bring life to others and to ourselves. With enough faith and enough willingness to work, we can make our dream come true.

As in opening our garden, the rewards lie in the risking. They are found in the doing. Those rewards include the discovery of fresh energy, new confidence, experience and joy. We discover what we are made of, and what we are capable of doing. But we need to make a beginning. Without that beginning those rich rewards remain only in our imagination, shelved, alongside the dream itself, in continuing isolation, safe from all that might damage and hurt us. By doing nothing, we isolate ourselves from all that can heal and recreate us. From this position we can only theorise from our beliefs, unable to back our theories with practical experience.

Occasionally we lose sight of our vision or dream, and become muddled and dispirited; this happens to Christians as well as to everyone else. A clergyman is expected by his parish to be full of fresh ideas. I know about this; I come from a clergy family and realise that the expectations of them are understandable, but often unrealistic and unreasonable. A clergyman is as likely as anyone else to have times when ideas will not come. Underneath each dog-collar, as underneath each business suit, breathes a human being with all the strengths and weaknesses, the hopes and fears of any other

81

person. The self-confident, able young curate may one day find that he lacks inspiration, and is frightened of preaching the sermon. If he is able to look at this problem with a friend or colleague, his understanding of himself will be deepened, his relationship with the other person will be strengthened, and in time he will have a clearer vision again.

If we are married, one of the best people to discuss such problems with is our partner. This will work provided we do not put each other on a pedestal. A clergyman who expects his wife to hang on his words every Sunday is being unrealistic. Equally, a woman who expects her husband to be the unfailing, noble orator, always inspiring, always in control of his material, is unrealistic too. Our dreams of each other need bringing down to earth to avoid long-term disenchantment. We need to talk to each other about them. This way we have more chances of finding a way forward.

One thing we do need to do is to exercise the giving and receiving of loving, honest criticism. I expected and hoped for constructive criticism from my husband and my producer after writing my draft scripts for Radio 4's 'Prayer for the Day'. Working together like this was enriching. I had grown to expect and fear the red correction pen from school days, with 'See me' at the bottom of my work. To discover that it was possible to work in an atmosphere of mutual encouragement, while learning to communicate was most rewarding.

It is important for our growth to take all the opportunities that present themselves to learn how to accept criticism and to handle times of dryness and failure, with honesty. It is wise, when choosing a friend or partner, to choose someone who understands these facets of human experience and can meet them. Not to acknowledge these feelings of dryness or failure can lead to self-deception and prevent us from growing healthily. Opening ourselves up to face these times, is a risk worth taking. We discover more about ourselves, and more about the love and acceptance of God. This helps us to feel less alone, and more alive.

Being alive is not about sitting still. It involves concentrated effort. We have to exert ourselves. Today we are led to believe from advertisements that life is easy and requires little effort.

We are persuaded that the less painful, less costly way is better. We are encouraged to be intellectually and spiritually lazy, little realising that life without cost is the way to apathy and death. So we sink into a form of sleeping sickness. We need to put ourselves into living, to give ourselves away a little, to die a little, if we want to go on growing. Growing is about discovering new potential.

Some while ago, I was encouraged to broadcast some 'Thoughts for the Day'. I received encouraging responses, and had enjoyed the experience. Strengthened by this I applied for a residential radio course where I could receive some intensive training; I wanted to improve and be more confident. I was warned about the pressure that members of the course were expected to undergo, and became increasingly anxious as the course grew nearer. Would I be able to stand it? What would happen if we all decided to go out to the pub together in the evening, where my old fear of crossing busy roads unaided would be confronted? But underneath all these anxieties, I knew I wanted to be a better broadcaster. I little realised that risking myself in this way would mean rewards outside the world of broadcasting.

At the course, eight of us gathered and prepared to start work. We were assigned our working partners for the week. My partner was Sister Rose, a nun from Uganda. Rose had a strong personality and plenty of guts. There was laughter in her musical voice, and she brought a lightness to the intensity of our work. As a group we became close and mutu-ally supportive. We worked till late each evening relaxing only over meals, which were gracious interludes when we could laugh over our mistakes, or sit in exhausted heaps. There was no time to go out for a walk, so my fears about the roads were allayed. Rose and I learned to splice and edit tape, to interview and be interviewed, to use machines and to write and deliver a script. We learnt to introduce records, to handle a studio 'phone-in', all leading up to the final climax of presenting our own twenty-minute programme. At the end of the week the tension and excitement was at its height, and

our programmes were as ready as they would ever be, to go
out on air on Radio Hatchend.

While Rose was preparing to present her programme, the
final and most demanding exercise, news came through of
her father's sudden death in Uganda. She was devastated,
and beside herself with grief. The whole building resounded
with her cries of agony and forsakenness. There was nothing
secretive about her reaction to the news. Everyone on the
course knew what had happened. But I was secretly anxious
that more involvement might be required of me, more than
I could handle. I was inexperienced when it came to bereavement and death. After all, I thought, the priest was with
her. Her cries continued, more desperately, and the group
suggested that I should go to Rose. So, knowing they were
right, but uncertain what I could offer, I knocked on the door
of the priest's room, and entered.

Seeing my new-found friend distraught, my self-conscious
anxiety disappeared, and I shut the door and knelt down
beside her, while the priest sat nearby. Rose allowed us to
stay with her while she worked out her grief, openly. Her
cries for her father reminded me of Christ's words, 'My God,
my God, why have you forsaken me?' To me, Rose was no
longer just a Roman Catholic nun. She was a young woman
who had just lost her beloved father. She had trusted two
other human beings with her deepest feelings, as if we had
been members of her own family. Though her face was stained
with tears, and her veil removed, her dignity was total. She
showed, in her trust, the deep dignity of a human being made
by God.

Rose had risked a good deal by being so open. She had
taught us much about real life, by allowing us to share her
experience in this way. By signing on to the radio course, I
had learned not only more about broadcasting, but understood more about a friend's grief in bereavement. There are
surprises when we launch out into something new, far beyond
our imagining.

The rewards of risking include not only wisdom and new

understanding, but also increased confidence, and a feeling that we are alive and significant. Launching out into something new can bring joy. Another kind of launch is finding the courage to use our talents for the first time. A retired cardiologist I knew was excited to have discovered that he had a talent for painting. Late in his life, this discovery has given him a new zest for living. He had always wanted to paint, but had been told at school that he had no artistic talent, so he had not thought it worth trying. Breaking the blank sheet of paper with a word, or daring to touch the virgin canvas with a dab or splodge of colour, is venturing. We need a renewed spirit of adventure to recover a sense of fun and excitement in God's creation.

Adventuring is exciting, and letting ourselves go a little, means we make room for new life to take root and spring. New energy flows in and we find enthusiam in making something happen. It is like learning to walk again, exciting but sometimes painful. It is important to take small steps as we cover new ground, and to build confidence gradually. As confidence begins to grow, we feel the energy and enthusiasm mounting, and then it is tempting to run, a little too early, and over-reach ourselves. A friend of mine had a hip operation, and as she was learning to walk again, her consultant gave her a piece of good advice. He said, 'Always do a little less than you think you can.' She followed this advice, and in time was able to walk quite freely.

In venturing out into new experiences, building confidence, finding courage and joy in living, we are wise to pause from time to time to review how we are doing. If we do not stop for a while we may lose a sense of balance and proportion. Regular review is good management practice, and refusing to review could indicate that there is something to hide or something we are afraid will come to light. There may be a genuine fear that we will lose control of our situation by pausing in this way. But if we do not pause to see how we are doing, our small steps can turn to thoughtless, untimely strides. We need to remember our particular gift from God, the ability to make choices and to say both 'Yes' and 'No'.

We need to know where the brakes are. Learning how to stop, or to say 'No', is a vital part of good, healthy living.

We are responsible for ourselves, for each other and for our world. Rushing forward into life may be exciting while the confidence lasts, but there comes a time for most of us, when there is an enforced stop. Ultimately the stop will be death, though as Christians we believe that this leads on to something greater. We need to discern when enough is enough. Over-excitement and over-stimulation, living for kicks, is something we are at liberty to choose. That is our privilege as human beings. But when we choose this way with our eyes open, we deny ourselves much deep and long-term joy and enrichment. Pausing to review is far from being the cautious approach. To take another look helps us to pace ourselves, to last the course, fully alive and confident. So pausing to review is not only about saying 'No'; it is an opportunity to say 'Yes' as well.

Saying 'Yes' means looking honestly at ourselves and wanting to see where our creative talents lie. There are so many possibilities. We may be able to paint, to cook, to listen or to speak; we may like to garden, visit someone's house, write letters or read aloud; we may be good with computers or woodwork, decorating, singing or climbing; we may enjoy asking questions or telling stories, speaking a foreign language or sculpting, dressmaking, accounting, being with children. The list is endless. If we want to, we will find something that we can do, or are already enjoying. Saying 'Yes' means giving space to ourselves to do what we want to do.

Saying 'Yes' and saying 'No' are part of responsible living, and pausing to review ourselves helps us to discern whether we are achieving a creative balance. Increasing numbers of people are seeing the wisdom of taking time out to go somewhere quiet on retreat, where, far from escaping from the world, they consider their position before God, regarding their relationships with family, friends and colleagues, reviewing their own lives. It is an opportunity to adjust the rhythm, to slow down and take control once more, and even to change direction. Like a precision instrument, our controls need tuning.

There are many people who cannot take time out for such a retreat. They are often people who care for others, or who have someone totally dependent on them. Mothers and single parents with small children, those caring for elderly or handi-capped relatives, find it difficult to make the time or raise the resources to make this possible. These people need special care and understanding. They need the attention of those of us with more time on our hands, who would be willing to take some of the strain of being on duty twenty-four hours a day. They do not need our advice, but often practical help – maybe baby- or granny-sitting and house-minding – while the carers claim some time and space for themselves, and choose their own kind of retreat. It might be to sleep, to walk or to take a ride to somewhere different. It needs to be a change of scene.

If we pack our lives with more and more new experiences without stopping to see where we are going, we begin to drift and lose our sense of direction. We need to learn to pause, to take stock, to review and to dream some more. Too much activity, too much unrelieved excitement will tire us, and dull our senses. Once our senses become dulled, then fear is muf-fled too. We become unable to discern a danger signal when we see one.

Just as too much activity and excitement can dull our senses, so too much reviewing can exhaust our opportunity to grow. A good gardener will know that if he digs up his plants repeatedly to look at the roots they will die. They need time to establish themselves, to acclimatise and settle to the business of growing. We are like that, and need space and privacy to flourish. But not too much, and not for too long. We need to find a creative balance, between being and doing, between stopping and continuing, and with all our responses alert, where we are unafraid to be.

Once I had begun to find new confidence flowing years ago, I ventured out of my home in east London, little by little. Still very fearful of shopping alone, I would let myself out gently, glad to hold on to my daughter's pram-handle for support. Later, in south London, I found the courage to drive short distances, sometimes going a little further afield to a favourite shop where I would buy myself a small present as a reward. Now I travel alone to London by train, and am able to face the busy roads and cross them, knowing that I can ask for help from another human being if I need it. I am a growing person. And as the confidence grows, the more exciting life becomes. The temptation to fly away from all that which requires hard work and concentrated effort is sometimes there, and my new-found freedom can become an occasion for selfish greed. This is where the review comes in. Pausing to thank God for the new sense of freedom is a major part of the process. Going on to decide what kind of life I want to lead is about looking at the present, the now, affirming what is good, noticing what is destructive, and deciding what to do next.

9

The Healing of Acceptance

Not facing the truth leads us to pretend, and this pretending can begin when we are quite young. As a seven-year-old, alone in hospital with a collapsed lung, I found it hard to accept that I was so ill. I was determined to be a bridesmaid at a family wedding at the end of the week. I wanted to be well for it. Only when my mother came to visit me, a few days before the wedding, with the news that I was not well enough to go, did I break down in tears, and accept the dreaded truth that I could not yet join my family. I then began to feel better, but only after the tears. Until then I had been living under the delusion that if I behaved well, and did what the nurses told me, and if I was 'good', then I would be 'good enough' and so better, and able to go to the wedding. Truth and behaviour had been confused, even in a small girl's mind. In the same way, our acceptability by God does not depend on our behaviour. It depends on whether we are facing the truth each day, about ourselves, about God, and about each other – accepting it wholeheartedly and without fearing that we will miss something important.

It will not be easy to understand the meaning of acceptance for ourselves until we have begun to identify moments when it has been part of our own experience, and when we have seen it active in others. If we have known constant accepting love through our growing years, then it will be easier for us than for those who have been less fortunate. Separation, divorce, sickness and death can make us feel deserted or forsaken, and will have undermined some of the original trust that we were born with. In defending ourselves we become a little suspicious of declarations of commitment, love or acceptance, and unwilling to trust ourselves in close relationships, without constant reassurance. As well as becoming suspicious, fearing more desertion, we also become angry. We blame those who leave us, and then, in our confusion, begin to blame ourselves.

Acceptance frees the spirit. Acknowledging that we are capable of loving behaviour becomes possible when we have felt loved and accepted. I can remember an occasion when, as a teenager, I feared disapproval and judgement, and was taken by surprise.

One day I went to a chemist to buy some rouge for the first time, knowing that my mother did not like wearing cosmetics herself, or seeing them applied heavily on other people. I was fair-skinned and had become tired of hearing friends and relations say how pale I looked. So it was with some trepidation that I sauntered into the garden, my cheeks slightly tinted, where she was hanging out some washing. I wanted to know if it showed, but felt too shy and anxious to ask outright, fearing her disapproval. Glancing at me she asked, 'Are you all right'? 'Yes, I'm fine. Why?' I replied. 'Oh, it's nothing,' she said, and continued pegging out the clothes. Curious by now, I said, 'Why did you ask'? and she paused. Leaving the washing for a moment, she turned and looked at me anxiously. 'You haven't got rouge on, have you?' she asked. With my heart pounding, I said, 'Yes'. Immediately she relaxed, smiled, and with some relief in her voice said, 'Thank goodness for that. I thought you had TB.'

Despite the great care I had taken in applying the rouge to my cheeks, my mother knew me too well, and I could not deceive her. Indeed I did not want to. I wanted to share my problem with her, and also my attempt to solve it. I wanted to know that my attempt was good enough for her, as it was good enough for me with that one proviso. Two small patches of pink on my cheeks filled her with more anxiety than whether I was wasting my money on fripperies, or pretending to be something I was not. Her relief was my relief. She wanted me to be well. Having half expected disapproval and judgement, I received acceptance. She did not tell me to remove the rouge, but advised me how to apply it more skilfully. She allowed me to be myself, living with my decision, and free from guilt. I wore my rouge with pride, and without fear. I felt free.

Experiences like this help to build confidence. They help us to believe that as we are, we are loved, lovable and good enough to be alive. They help us to relate to one another with dignity. But even with plenty of good experiences, there come times later in life when we become again like confused teen-agers, uncertain of ourselves underneath the bravado.

As a newcomer to Liverpool, I was uncertain what my role would be as the new bishop's wife. I was aware of my limitations, yet keen to show willing. I had made up my mind to do what I enjoyed. I resolved that, whenever possible, I would visit the homes of clergy families informally, as I had done as a suffragan bishop's wife in Southwark. It was appreciated there, and I trusted that it would be appreciated in the North too. I told someone more established in the diocese of my intention. 'Oh!,' she said, 'You can't do that up here. They wouldn't understand. People like to have warning before the bishop's wife calls.' I felt badly put down. For a moment I felt utterly useless, and 'not good enough'. I had allowed myself to slip back into dependence on another's approval. Instead of trusting my own judgement, I abandoned myself to someone else's opinion of me, inwardly cowering, instead of sticking to my own point of view, although I believed it to be valid. At first I did not include this informal visiting in my work and I regretted it for some time. Now, I trust my own judgement, and feel quite free to visit some homes informally – and have always received a welcome. This welcome, this acceptance, remains important to me. We need to relate positively with other people.

It is easier to accept the truth when we know we are not alone. When facing difficulties, we need the grace of another's accepting presence. We need someone there when we are hurting. That someone can be on the end of a telephone, living next door, at home, or in a consulting room. Years ago when I discovered that I could not walk outside my front door alone, or go shopping like other people, I made matters worse by blaming myself for not finding my own resources, or for not having enough faith to overcome this awkward disability. I was angry with myself for not being perfect, and, in effect, I shut myself out from others. But I was fortunate to be living in a friendly community. Although many of the people there did not fully understand what was happening to me, they accepted me as I was. My family were equally accepting, though puzzled. My doctor did not patronise me, and last, but not least, my husband went on loving me, difficult as it was for him to accept or understand. He stood by me while I struggled to rebuild my self-confidence. Professional and lay people, family and friends, all had a measure of confidence in me, which enabled me to do my own work in a loving environment. It was an atmosphere of grace. No one told me to pull myself together, or snap out of it. No one told me how selfish I was. I told myself these things, expecting others to join in. But they did not. Instead, they stood by me and prayed for my healing, little realising that they were part of the healing process. Nothing made me want to live and to be whole more than the knowledge that I was loved, needed and accepted, and was not alone.

Part of the truth is difficult to accept. It is the part which reminds us that we are not yet whole or complete, and which reminds us that we are vulnerable. The fear of death stalks us until we accept that this is part of what it means to be alive. We need to discover how to live the short span that we have to the fullest extent.

To do this, we need people who accept us as we are, confused, angry and hurt. True acceptance will allow for our humanity, without judging or adding to our feelings of guilt. We need assurance that what we are, and so what we feel, is not wrong, but human. It is not wrong to be human. It is because of our inability to accept one another that we become afraid – we fear judgement and punishment. Because we are not yet whole, either as individuals or communities, we need to find ways of living with our incompleteness, and of helping ourselves and each other to live through those times of fear.

There is a place for judgement and punishment, but they need to be seen as part of a more complete picture. Many images of God portray him as a stern unmerciful judge only concerned with condemnation. This makes us feel throughout our lives that we are in the dock, fearfully awaiting our sentence. This partial picture of God's nature leaves out the crucial coming of Christ, when a loving and human image was introduced. Christ's coming showed that God recognised our humanity and the feelings that accompany it. His coming also showed that we are acceptable and loved by God, and have the resources to create love and life in relationship with one another. The distant picture of the unmerciful judge is transformed. A new picture comes into view where we see a person who can both cry and shout with anger, who wants to mix with hurt people and those of doubtful reputation, yet without condoning their actions. Like placing one transparency over another, our picture of God comes together, producing both a righteous and merciful judge and a person who knows about suffering.

Holding these two images of God apart we confuse and distort his nature. This in turn causes our understanding of ourselves to be confused as well. Dominant parents, teachers and other authority figures in our childhood reinforce our picture of the stern judgement of God, and we develop into unbalanced, fear-driven human beings who expect rejection at every turn, and who feel safe only when relating to a rule book of behaviour. We go on to reject and condemn ourselves and each other, by banishing the bits we would rather not own, as if they did not exist. This contributes to a destructive way of life where we damage not only ourselves but others as well.

It is damaging to deny disturbing feelings. It is even more damaging to condemn them. Feeling angry with someone is not wrong, but nursing that anger in private becomes destructive. Falling in love with someone else's wife is not wrong, but nurturing that feeling in private leads to irresponsible actions which break up another person's life. Accepting the feelings of anger and love is truthful behaviour, and provides a better chance of showing that we are made in the image of God. Following this acceptance, we have the opportunity to do something creative with those feelings.

Holding the two images of God together, we find that though he is Judge, he is a merciful one, and though he is a human and loving Saviour, he is not soft and indecisive. Accepting God like this helps us to accept ourselves, as well as one another.

There is no need to go on being confused. As soon as we believe in our heart of hearts that it is not wrong to feel angry, to feel guilty, to feel hurt, or to feel afraid, then we are well on the way to understanding ourselves. We will go on to understand and accept others who express these feelings. We need to be accepted, and we need to accept each other just as we are.

For many years I felt unable to accept that being afraid was all right. I used to believe that Christians, especially, should be free from fear, and that any signs of it reappearing were signs of weakness, which made me feel guilty for letting Christ down. In my confusion, I thought that my fears were signs of disobedience or sin, and should be punished. So I began to apologise for being afraid, to God in my prayers, and in a way, to myself. I went on to believe, rather deeply, that I was not good enough. I was not good enough for God, for my husband, for any friends I would make, and not a good enough mother for my daughter. This craving for perfection was unhealthy and damaging. Learning to accept myself as God accepts me has taken time. Just as the sun rises each morning, slowly but surely a realisation has dawned that I am acceptable, loved even, just as I am, imperfect but alive. Talking about being loved or accepted was not enough. I had to believe it, and let it sink in until it was part of my own experience.

But I am not alone in this. Many Christians are confused about what is acceptable to God. We have allowed ourselves mistakenly to believe that Christianity is primarily about good behaviour. But behaviour is about what we do and not about how we feel. God accepts us as we are. Christ's coming meant that we have a pattern of how to manage our God-given humanity. He knew anger and fear like the rest of us, and went on to show us that we have the resources to handle feelings like that without doing wrong. He showed us how.

In talking about forgiveness, Christ also demonstrated that he knew we would not be perfect, and that we would hurt one another. He knew that there are ways of changing our behaviour to be more loving rather than less loving, to be more accepting rather than less so, and to be more creative and less destructive. But he left us to choose which way we want to go. Christ did not come to moralise, or to repeat the ten commandments. He came to show us what God was like. He came to show us the meaning of love, to show us that God loves and accepts us as he made us, and that he stays with us through suffering, through deliberate wrong-doing or sin, helping us to learn to practise forgiveness and to change our ways, becoming more loving human beings. He came to show us the way to wholeness and healing. But we still need to choose which way we want to go, how we want to behave, and what we want to do. God will not impose that on us. That way we would lose our essential dignity. Christ came to make it plain that God loves us and that we are designed to create and to love one another as he does.

When the church or individual Christians rush to judge themselves, or each other, or others outside the church, then we lose the possibility of loving, replacing it with feelings of guilt and fear. The world outside is deterred by the apparent double standards of those within the Church when we preach love and acceptance on the one hand, but practise judgement on the other. Christ did not come to moralise; he came to be with us, by accepting our humanity, and sharing in the painful parts of our growth. This is where the Church should be too. The people Christ criticised were the hypocrites, and those who pretended to be more whole than they were. He exhorted people to face the truth about themselves.

It was disturbing to witness, on a recent ecumenical visit to South Africa, a will among so many white people to stay separated from their black brothers and sisters. On the other hand, listening to black people, it was clear that they do not feel complete without white people, and regard the enforced segregation as damaging to everyone in that beautiful country.

Some find it easier to accept and trust than others. Trying to find a way of accepting more and judging less, takes time, and depends on our experience. Someone with a history of physical or emotional abuse will find it harder to trust or accept other people than the person who has not had these experiences. Equally, someone who has known constant love, and not had fear as a driving force in their upbringing, will have difficulty in understanding those who are harsh in their judgement, or even cruel in their actions. Somewhere in between, lie all the rest of us, a little lacking in self-confidence, and too ready to look for criticism and judgement.

People who give me the impression of being powerful, controlled and organised, through no fault of their own, present me with a problem. When someone like that comes to stay, I find it hard to control the urge to tidy up; for some reason, our home does not feel good enough for them. There are others with whom there's no problem, and I relax more. They make me feel that they are glad to see us, even when we are in a mess, or clearly not in complete control. I feel accepted, not judged. I feel freed from seeking approval. When I feel that my home is not good enough for visitors it is, more accurately, me not feeling good enough for them.

So the problem of acceptance or rejection does not lie with my visitors; it lies within me. If I have not decided that my home is good enough, then I lay the way open for disapproval and judgement. Not positively accepting my home as it is, and not positively accepting myself as I am, provide this foothold for fear to get a grip, propelling me to change things, for the wrong reason. So, it is vital for our well-being, to notice who we are, and what motivates us.

If we discover that we are afraid of rejection and judgement, we shall be restless people, unable to be still for long, always needing to build up our store of achievements to prove something to ourselves and to others. We also expect others to store up achievements, and to behave well, before we allow ourselves to accept them, rather like an ambitious schoolmaster more anxious about keeping his position than whether his pupil is ready to learn. The more we are dissatisfied with ourselves, the more we shall look for achievements in others. We begin to live in other people's lives. If someone close to us does not appear to achieve much, it is tempting to push them until they do, and in doing so feed our own starved ego.

This can happen quite unawares. Parents push their children, wives push their husbands, teachers pressurise their pupils, all motivated by their own lack of fulfilment and confidence. This is clearly damaging, and needs to be overcome if we are to relate to others and to live with them in wholeness and harmony.

One element of this harmony lies in the way we treat each other – if we are to accept and be accepted, we need to be sensitive and courteous.

However, good manners are just superficial gloss unless they are underpinned with a genuine desire to accept the other person as they are, giving them space to be themselves. Really good manners are the result of loving and accepting one another as human beings, and not just a mechanical action or a recipe for civilised living. Someone with impeccable manners, outwardly showing respect and acceptance for another is quite capable of damaging them in other ways. This kind of pretence is not true courtesy or good manners at all. Gracious behaviour will be the result of a genuine desire to be with, and be acquainted with, another person.

To accept other people is to welcome them as they are, without trying to change them. This is not to be confused with a disinterested resignation. Accepting someone, is to remain interested in them, believing them to have good reason for acting the way they do. It is respecting their integrity, even though we may disagree with their ideas. When a person turns to dealing in drugs, or to crime, he must be brought to justice. But to stop there would be to contribute to his disintegration. To respect a person means that we will want to know why they acted the way they did. Finding a good reason does not condone their actions, but leaves it to the judge in court to do the judging and us free to relate as fellow human beings who also hurt other people, and who have the power to heal those hurts. That is why we need to respect and support not only the judiciary, but also those who work in the probation service, in social work, and in work involving the resettlement of offenders. These people are engaged in accepting those who have fallen foul of the law, while they are being punished.

There are many people in our communities who are not criminals, yet we reject and condemn them as if they were. For some years I have been involved with the Liverpool Family Service Unit, the local branch of a national voluntary organisation that began during the 1939–45 war. Conditions for many families had been very bad for years, and the war brought these conditions to light; many families found themselves unable to manage. Their resources dwindled, and sickness, poverty, loneliness and bereavement took them to their limits. The Family Service Units (F.S.U.) were formed to offer friendship and a helping hand to families in this kind of need.

Families today still suffer chronically from multiple problems, and the F.S.U. offers help without punishing attitudes. The workers do not blame a family for being poor, sick, or unemployed. Every family they work with is free to ask them to leave, and so retain some personal dignity and control over their own lives, however fragmented. As well as bringing their friendship and time, the workers bring skills in social work, counselling, therapy and family support.

Voluntary organisations like the F.S.U. provide many people with the possibility of feeling accepted as human beings, and prevent them from feeling totally rejected and punished for being poor or inadequate by parts of the community to which they belong. They begin to learn to trust again. Accepted by others, they can accept themselves.

Certainly the acceptance of others has helped me reach the point of self-acceptance. It means that, in driving for example, I have had to be patient, inching my way forward, from short distances to more ambitious journeys. I learned to be satisfied with each small sign of progress; in this way fear was brought back under control, in its rightful place. Now I enjoy driving, on busy dual carriageways through London in the rush hour, and daily in Liverpool – I have only recently driven on a motorway for the first time. My husband's genuine acceptance of the facts, and his own enjoyment of driving, has helped to make my progress steady and real. He has given me the grace of acceptance, which has been without accusation or impatience, leaving me free to decide to return to driving at my own pace, and without pressure. In turn I have had to learn to accept graciously my husband's willingness to offer to drive on motorways, refusing to feel guilty for not taking a fuller share of the driving.

This unpressurising acceptance is undeserved, unconditional, and with no strings attached. In my case this grace is found in another person who loves me. It often makes me ask what I have done to deserve this kind of loving. The answer is, 'Nothing at all.' The knowledge that I am loved for myself without having to earn that love is often beyond me, and too wonderful to understand. But I know it is there, in my husband, and that it is a sign of God's love for me, and does not depend on whether I can drive on motorways.

When we begin to trust again after losing confidence in ourselves or in others, we will have found firmer ground to stand on. We trust other people more when they do not betray us or leave suddenly without warning. We begin to trust ourselves when we are able to accept, without running away, the truth about who we are as it unfolds. But our humanity causes us to lose faith in ourselves and in others sometimes, so it is important to seek for deeper truth to undergird us when we fail.

In my kitchen there is a lot of wall space. I like to put up pictures, cartoons, postcards and newspaper cuttings. One day a church newspaper headline caught my eye. So I cut it out and stuck it to one of my cupboards as a constant reminder. It said, 'God accepts us just as we are.' The truth proclaimed by that headline has provided me with a sense of support and encouragement for many years. It has also challenged my understanding of what kind of God I believe in.

Looking beyond the tangible takes us to spiritual truths about a living God, who loves us just as we are, and who through Christ understands the human feeling of betrayal and death and yet forgives. When we are able to believe this, it becomes easier to trust again. If we keep looking, believing his Spirit to be somewhere in us, in others and the whole of creation, we shall find him in a thousand places. There will be less reason to be afraid.

10

The Gift of Grace

We need the grace of acceptance, as this helps us to feel understood. This word 'grace' often appears in our Christian worship, and not so often in ordinary, everyday conversation. It is a much under-used word, and I am not convinced that we have stopped to think for very long about its meaning. When we say the words of the Grace, we say, 'The grace of our Lord Jesus Christ, and the love of God, and the fellowship of the Holy Spirit be with us all.' Are we, I wonder, aware of what we are saying, or are we just vaguely wishing something good for each other.

I believe it is time to use the word 'grace' more often. Then we would find we are experiencing it more naturally. For example a baby at the breast experiences grace through his mother's milk. It is plentiful, nourishing, unconditional, and part of the mother's loving action. Or an infant, after having a tantrum, receives grace in the embrace of his parent when it is all over. He knows that he is still loved, still accepted, even after stamping his feet in anger and frustration. The embrace is unconditional, undeserved, and offered in love. The teenager, after shouting at his parents and walking out, knows the meaning of grace when they welcome him back with no recrimination. In the same way, as adults, we can bring comfort to one another, mercy and accepting love. Grace is a gift, free and constantly on offer, whoever we are, and whatever we have done, and it is waiting to be both given and received.

But a gift is not a gift until it is received. Receiving signifies a whole relationship. Someone who offers grace is someone who loves, and who hopes, indeed longs, for a loving relationship with the recipient, yet does not count on it. In this kind of relationship there is no pressure, coercion or manipulation to love, for that would be a contradiction in terms. There is no 'I'll give my life for you, so that you will love me,' but rather, 'I will die for you because I want you to know how much I love you.' The giver of grace does not blame the object of his love for refusing his gift, but goes on offering it, whatever the response, right up to the end. Receiving or accepting another's gift of grace or love is just as important to the relationship as the giving.

The trouble is that none of us is complete yet. God's grace is pure, whereas ours is a pale reflection of the depth of his acceptance and love. Because we let each other down, and fear betrayal, we sometimes refuse an offer of grace, or fail to recognise it. In our desperate attempts to be independent, sometimes competing with one another, we turn down small offers of grace or loving behaviour, and so refuse the possibility of building, in the long run, more gracious, more loving and cohesive relationships. We cultivate a habit of ungraciousness, afraid of giving way.

Accepting a gift puts us in another's debt. In this business-orientated society, we become conditioned to the idea that receiving something for nothing is not profitable. Our giving is in danger of turning into a transaction. So we become afraid to either give or receive gifts until we are sure that the message is clear. There are occasions when it is wise to refuse a gift. If we suspect an element of blackmail in the offer, then we should be suspicious.

But the fear of an ulterior motive in another prevents trust from forming. A woman I knew, who had grown up in a tradition of sharing, was one day making some jam and, because it was her neighbour's birthday, she put a small pot together with a card on her neighbour's doorstep. But her neighbour was disturbed; she had grown up in a different tradition, where there was very little trust, and she became suspicious. She thought this was a bribe, and suspected the woman would want something from her in the future. She had a history of physical and emotional abuse, and had grown to mistrust most people. She was not used to being loved unconditionally.

With God there is no such ulterior motive, no strings attached. He loves us with a pure love that has no wish to dominate, manipulate or coerce us into a loving relationship with him. He loves, he waits, and leaves us to respond when we are ready. But he goes on loving, whatever our response.

There are signs of God's grace all around us. We find these signs in people and in the rest of creation. There are people who by their attitudes give us a sense that there is room to breathe and to be ourselves. They help us to feel released from the claustrophobic pressure that makes us feel judged and sentenced. They are instruments of God's grace, as we all can be, with the power to heal, to make whole, or to liberate others.

God's grace is present in nature, in all forms of art, and in our own minds. It can be evoked by sounds, by sights and by touch, which remind us of earlier good experiences. For example the smell of freshly cut wood chips brings life to me as it reminds me of the unhurried walks that I enjoyed with my family years ago. The smell of lavender reminds me that I'm loved because my first boy-friend gave me a bottle of lavender water on my birthday when I was thirteen. The sound of a cockney voice reminds me of our time in east London and the warmth, humour and friendship that we experienced in the middle of some difficult times. The sound of Bach's B minor Mass, or of a jazz piano, evoke other memories which give me a sense of wholeness, release and well-being. The sound of a Liverpool voice makes me feel at home and want to smile. We are surrounded by reminders of God's unconditional love, as well as being channels of his grace ourselves.

Essentially, God's grace is to be found in reading the Bible, in prayer and in private and public worship. God's grace can also be recognised in our hospitals, through the actions of reliable, sensitive hospital staff. The patients who receive their service trustingly, find their fears alleviated and are helped back to physical or mental health, or to face long-term ill health, pain or even death.

103

Unconditional love, or grace, is not like an anaesthetic, imposing a false sense of calm when there is pain. Neither is it like a stiff drink which puts distance between us and our sorrows! The presence of grace helps us *in* our infirmities, *while* we are suffering, and *during* times of great fear, to face what is happening. Grace comes to help in time of need. Grace does not threaten, but provides the space that an imprisoned person needs, the air that a suffocating person needs, the blood that a dying person needs. We need to recognise the signs of grace, as they are very close to us, and we often take them for granted. These signs of grace can be found in our everyday lives, and in people most of all.

Because I love singing, I joined a choir in Liverpool. Over the years, my confidence in public places has greatly increased, but each time we came near to a concert, I became anxious and wondered whether I could cope with a public performance, even though I was only one of many singers. As the formal occasion approached, I would find it difficult to finish my meal beforehand, and my mouth would go dry. Once in our places ready to begin, my muscles would tighten, as if I was preparing to be hit by something. During the concert, it would take a good deal of concentration to combine singing and keeping my eye on the baton, with remembering to relax the taut muscles in my legs, knees and neck. I would often experience a terrifying panic in the middle of the quietest moment, when I would feel dizzy and hot, fearing that I would disgrace myself and upset the performance by sitting down, walking out or fainting. I was much too proud to sit down or leave.

One day I decided that I could not continue like this, as though nothing was happening. So I confided in the singers nearest to me, people I felt I could trust. I asked one of them if I could take her arm if I needed it, and she readily agreed. After that I felt much less alone. Several performances later, I discovered my problem had eased. Sharing it had helped; I had needed to take my friend's arm once. I began to look forward to singing in the concerts instead of dreading them.

Months later we performed the Verdi Requiem, which I have loved for years. It is an emotional piece, and I knew I would be caught up in the music. That night was a triumph. I enjoyed every moment. The fear had evaporated, and I did not need to take my friend's arm. Her willingness to accept me with my fear was, to me, a true sign of grace.

Because of the habitual fear of years, I have approached subsequent concerts with some caution, but I know that my friends are there, sharing my problem. To be able to swallow pride, and admit a need, is to find grace. A choir is like life; we are not there to sing solos, but to support one another, bringing our different voices and talents to produce something creative together.

With this kind of mutual support, we can keep our dignity, because we will be able to share our ability to heal through mutual acceptance. In each of us there lies a supply of grace, and a supply of mercy, providing between us all that is necessary to show what the love of God is really like. We are left with the will to choose whether or not to tap these resources and put our faith to work.

A different kind of support is provided by those who prepare food in our homes, schools, restaurants and cafes. Every day they provide strength and nourishment for our bodies; they are instruments and signs of grace, enabling us to be alive and taking a full part in the whole of creation. Saying 'Thank you' or saying Grace before or after meals has sadly gone out of fashion; it is good to acknowledge God and those who have prepared the food. Stopping for a cup of tea or a shared meal helps us to face one another, to relax together. Unconditional love, or grace, is like a cup of tea during a busy morning. It is not so different from the cup of cold water that Christ mentioned when he was talking to his disciples, teaching them how to love one another more fully.

Cups of tea, or cups of water, provide opportunities to pause in what we are doing, and to give time and space to ourselves, and to each other. But there are many in our world who do not have much more than a cup of polluted water. We do not offer them anything better. There are those nearer to us who are in poor health, without families, homes or work to give them dignity. The gifts and the grace of God seem to have departed from their lives. But freedom, health and growth are there to be shared. When we remain separated, we deny ourselves the means of grace that flow from those on whom we have turned our backs. We label some of our fellow human beings hooligans, or vandals, as if they were parcels ready for despatch; out of fear that they may spoil what control we have over our own lives, we pretend we can get on with living as if they did not exist.

Then again, many of us treat mentally handicapped people like that, yet they have so much to offer us, as those who work with them will testify. Their honesty and love can be disturbing, and frightens some people; yet facing the fear, and coming near, we find the grace of acceptance in people whom we had been tempted to banish.

We need to find ways of acknowledging that we belong to one another. Despatching any group of people by labelling them and turning our backs on them, we become the poorer. Black people, poor people, prisoners, and people with AIDS, have much to teach us about love and acceptance. We deprive ourselves if we allow fear to drive us apart, so that we have nothing to do with certain groups of the human race; and we lose our integrity.

If we settle for divisions, if we are unwilling to reach a hand across the divide, if we do not offer grace – we will not receive it. We will experience a hardening which is far more dangerous to us than the fantasy dangers that divide us. Hardness of heart is the opposite of grace; it is that self-imposed separation from God which is the greatest fear. We sometimes call it Hell. It is not imposed on us against our will; if we harden our hearts against our fellow human beings, we cut off the means of supply of grace and of life through our own choice. In the same way, if we shut our eyes to those parts of our own lives that we fear, we become divided, disintegrated, and then hardened; it will become increasingly impossible for us to be whole. If we want to go on growing more whole, developing together, we need to keep watch over ourselves. We need forgiving, understanding friends to help us change to a more loving way.

The hardening of hearts can happen between individuals in our own homes, and also between communities. This refusal to accept each other as we are leads to real separation and real misery. Where one person says to another, 'I never really knew you,' or 'You are not the person I married,' this indicates that a relationship is fractured and in danger of dying. If we practise this on a larger scale, we are inviting the same kind of consequence, which has far-reaching effects in our world. The cold war, the iron curtain, apartheid, endless wars around the globe are the reflection of individual behaviour.

When we harden our hearts it is often because we have been hurt or felt threatened. When someone we care for dies or leaves us, it hurts, so we steel ourselves against it happening or hurting again. After a while, the grace of time helps us to take courage to risk ourselves again, in another relationship. But if we feel hurt or betrayed by someone who is still close to us, we have the choice either to harden our hearts or to forgive.

Choosing to forgive is vital for wholeness. It makes all the difference to whether we blossom and flourish, growing healthy and loving, or whether we grow into bitter, withered and twisted people who gradually lose the capacity for living a full and rewarding life. The hurt we felt will turn to anger, and we will begin to hurt other people in return, contributing to a destructive way of life.

Choosing to forgive is part of being a growing person. But it can be very hard to do. Equally, being forgiven is part of the same important process and can be just as difficult. Doing the forgiving only implies we never hurt people and have no reason to receive forgiveness ourselves. This makes us patronising and aloof, unaware of what holds us together as human beings. It is like a priest who spends a great deal of his time hearing confessions and pronouncing absolution, and very little on making his own confession, or seeking forgiveness for himself from another person in an everyday relationship. He will find it hard to understand someone who feels hurt by his actions. I used to be like that, unaware that while speaking as a Christian student to individuals and groups about Christ's forgiveness for everyone, I was responsible for hurting those close to me. As a young Christian, when I was criticised, I would immediately claim Christ's forgiveness in private before looking at the hurt I had caused with the person concerned. Claiming forgiveness like this did not help me to become responsible for my hurtful actions. I shifted the responsibility onto Christ, separating him somehow from real life and real people, and moved on. All my good actions I attributed to Christ, and the harmful ones to the devil. The small hurts I put down to human weakness. The responsible, flesh and blood human being that I could have been became overlaid with beliefs and ideas, and failed to connect with reality. An important part of growing was being interrupted. It was no wonder I built a reputation as a student for being too good to be true, even among some of my friends.

In order to understand forgiveness we need to be sufficiently close to people who will tell us when we hurt them. Throwing bricks at each other as children in the play pen, is one way to learn to hurt and be hurt, but the more sophisticated ways of hurting come later, when we begin to master words and learn to manipulate other people. It is not usually difficult to be aware of physical hurt, because it shows, in cuts and bruises. But emotional damage is just as hurtful and needs to be checked. Whether we hurt, or do the hurting, there is still a need for healing. Experiencing this need for wholeness, we will welcome anything that can help to bring it about. Grace can offer that healing.

We need grace, when learning to forgive. Grace is a gift, to be received, and offered. It will not appear magically from the air. The signs are all around, both in people and in creation as a whole. When we find it difficult to forgive, it helps to remember how much we are loved by our Maker and, if we are fortunate, by those close to us. By receiving this love for ourselves, we will find the grace already there, to forgive those who hurt us. Sometimes the hurt is deep and takes longer to forgive completely. This is when it becomes even more important to love ourselves, as well as just loving those who love us. It is important, because there may be times when we feel quite alone, and it helps to be able to own everything that we are, all the feelings, all the actions, inside the loneliness. We shall then be owning to a common humanity with the one who has hurt us. Finding something in common will help to prevent us from feeling cut off and separated from each other. It will help us to feel less fearful, more self-confident, and more ready to love and forgive. We will remember that we too have the power to hurt, as well as to heal, and will find ourselves closer to the person who has hurt us, more able to accept them as they are. We cannot afford to be separated, and forgiving brings us closer.

But often, because of our pride and the fear of losing our dignity, we stand off and prefer to send out messages that we are not in need at all. Yet in our streets, under every roof, live other human beings like ourselves, who are in need. We all have needs; we are not alone. If we have lost faith in one another, then we need to ask why.

By nature, I am quite a self-contained person, and like time and space in which to be private. Only when I was ill or broken years ago, did I realise that healing began to come from admitting my need, losing some of my control, and letting go to others, who were there, offering love and skill. Only when I accepted their help, did I begin to feel more whole, more free and more human.

Later, when I was able to acknowledge my fear of losing control of my life by dying from cancer, I agreed to a course of radiotherapy. I determined to do all in my power to assist the professionals, and only then did I find the courage to lie there under those powerful rays, believing in their power to destroy the marauding cells. After this, I joyfully accepted the grace of my husband's constant and practical love while he nursed me back to health.

But this book is not about how to be healed from break-downs or cancer. Nor is it a catalogue of how many fears we can collect to show how brave we can be. I have been trying to show that there is a way to experience love and wholeness. Accepting that we are all human, frail and vulnerable, means that we open the door to receive the loving that is there to heal, in one another. In sharing my aspect of fear, I have wanted to create a greater freedom to give and receive love with all its healing power. Small fears are real fears, and are part of being alive. 'Silly fears' are real fears, and are not silly at all. Accepting that we have them is a way of loving ourselves. We can then go on to love our neighbour by sharing more openly with one another. This means that we are on the road to life, full of creativity, and wholeness. This is not a soft option, as there is work to do. But it is a challenge that we can face together. Alone and fragmented, we shall remain broken and diseased and increasingly fearful. Together and integrated, we shall find healing and love through one another, but only if that is what we really want.

Where, finally, can we find the strength to master our fears, to achieve wholeness? There is a place. It is where we all can go before our health begins to fail more seriously. It is very near, and is the place where we can tell each other about our fears of growing old, of losing our loved ones, of losing our health. It is the place where we can talk about being afraid of running into debt, of hitting our children or of harming ourselves. It is the place where we can share together that we fear losing the power to love, to have children, or to be successful. It is a place where we bring our hurts, and find acceptance and love, and where we are enabled to feel better, and glad to be alive. It is a place where we do not feel ashamed of our fears, and where we can find courage to take action, knowing we shall not be alone. This place is the Throne of Grace. It is where God is, and is a place of prayer. I believe that God is with us, firmly rooted, in the whole of creation, and in each other. Finding ways of meeting him in simple communication, we shall find we are loved, and healed and, inch by inch, delivered from the grip of our fears. We just need the will to be free, the courage to take the first step, and the faith to continue.

Coming to this place does not cost money. It means giving our lives, little by little, and involves courage. This kind of service transcends every high brick wall, and every hedge and barrier, and is offered through telephones, mail boxes, and in ordinary conversations. Wherever there are two or more people, grace is there. There is no dramatic claim of instant physical healing, but there is the continuing presence of the spirit of Christ, which provides love, acceptance and grace. With this grace we can not only help each other; we can face our fears together without pretence, and become what God meant us to be, loving, creative and fully alive. The choice is ours.

May the Grace of our Lord Jesus Christ,
and the Love of God,
and the Fellowship of the Holy Spirit
be with us all
this day, and for evermore.